Germany's Economic Renaissance

Germany's Economic Renaissance

Lessons for the United States

Jack Ewing

First published in 2014 by PALGRAVE MACMILLAN® in the United States—a division of St. Martin's Press LLC, 175 Fifth Avenue, New York, NY 10010.

Where this book is distributed in the UK, Europe, and the rest of the world, this is by Palgrave Macmillan, a division of Macmillan Publishers Limited, registered in England, company number 785998, of Houndmills, Basingstoke, Hampshire RG21 6XS.

Palgrave Macmillan is the global academic imprint of the above companies and has companies and representatives throughout the world.

Palgrave® and Macmillan® are registered trademarks in the United States, the United Kingdom, Europe and other countries.

ISBN: 978-1-137-34973-6

Library of Congress Cataloging-in-Publication Data

Ewing, Jack.
    Germany's economic renaissance : lessons for the United States / by Jack Ewing.
       pages cm
    Includes bibliographical references and index.
    ISBN 978-1-137-34973-6 (hardback)
      1. Industrial policy—Germany. 2. Small business—Germany. 3. International business enterprises—Germany. 4. Manpower policy—Germany. I. Title.
HD3616.G4E95 2014
338.0943—dc23

                                                                2013039979

A catalogue record of the book is available from the British Library.

Design by Amnet.

First edition: April 2014

10 9 8 7 6 5 4 3 2 1

To Zita Lee, my mother, who encouraged my interest in writing and will always be a model of patience, selflessness, and fortitude.

Contents

Introduction

Not so long ago, it looked as if Germany was slouching toward global irrelevance. Its once powerful economy was sagging under the burden of the welfare state. German workers were expensive and hard to fire. Unions were powerful and inflexible, with the power to set wages for whole industries. Taxes were high and rising, draining more than 37 percent of gross domestic product (GDP) by the end of the 1990.[1] Unemployment rose steadily through 2006, to more than 12 percent.[2] Domestic demand was shrinking as the birthrate fell and the number of retirees rose. Germany had no reply to the entrepreneurial energy of Silicon Valley and was a bystander in the development of the Internet. As America converted to a service economy and outsourced production to China, German managers—engineers, as a rule, rather than MBAs—clung to manufacturing, a strategy that seemed anachronistic and foolish. The fall of the Berlin Wall and the reunification of Germany, one of the only truly joyous moments in twentieth-century German history, gave way to the realization that the East German economy was bankrupt and grossly inefficient, and would take years and trillions of deutsche marks to become competitive. And with the end of the Cold War, Berlin was no longer a locus of geopolitical tension. If Germany was also a fading economic power, diplomats in a world no longer divided by the Iron Curtain could safely ignore it. By the beginning of the new millennium, the postwar economic miracle, the *Wirtschaftswunder*, seemed like a distant memory.

Yet less than a decade later, the country rebounded. German workers were still expensive, and taxes among the highest in the world. But the refusal to give up on old-fashioned metal banging now seemed like wise policy. German unemployment fell while joblessness rose in other developed countries, including America, which had become too dependent on real estate and financial services for growth. In 2012, Germany was a close third behind China and the United States among the world's largest exporters of merchandise. Germany, with about 81 million people, sold almost as many goods abroad as the United States, with about 314 million.[3] With just 6 percent of the population of China, Germany generated exports equal to more than 70 percent of what China produced for overseas consumption. As the eurozone debt crisis devastated nearby countries like Spain and Italy, Germany remained supremely aloof. In the most prosperous regions like Bavaria or Baden-Württemberg, there was full employment. The Bavarian city of Ingolstadt, the home of automaker Audi, had a jobless rate of less than 3 percent in 2012, and this was in the midst of recession in the rest of the eurozone. Nationwide, the unemployment rate had been cut in half. It was not an exaggeration to say that Germany had created a second *Wirtschaftswunder.*

Why? What allowed Germany to revive its economy in an amazingly short time? And what can America and other developed and developing nations learn from Germany's example?

The answer holds lessons for managers and policymakers in the United States and any other economy that is trying to revive or build a manufacturing base, which, as the unfortunate citizens of cities like Detroit can testify, is indispensable to a balanced economy with low unemployment. It holds lessons for managers wondering how they can compete with Chinese companies that pay their workers one-tenth as much as American workers earn.

In Germany, part of the credit for the country's rebound goes to household names like Audi, BMW and Daimler. They invested in China and other emerging countries at the right moment. They used automation to compensate for high labor costs in Germany, and judiciously relocated some production to Eastern Europe or Asia. At the same time, they were careful to keep research and development and intellectual property close to home. German companies dominated the global market for premium automobiles even as competitors like Fiat, Ford of Europe or General Motors' Opel unit accumulated huge losses on the Continent.

German policymakers also deserve some of the credit. Under Chancellor Gerhard Schröder, a Social Democrat and nominally a socialist, the German government addressed some, though not all, of the rigid labor regulations that made it so difficult for German companies to respond to fluctuations in demand. Under Schröder's successor, Angela Merkel, Germany cut the basic corporate tax rate to 15 percent from 25 percent, well below the 35 percent rate in the United States.[4] (The total tax burden in Germany is still greater, because of higher personal income taxes, value-added taxes, and other levies.) Even labor unions deserve a share of the praise. While they often talk tough, German labor leaders rarely stage massive strikes and are fundamentally pragmatic. They allowed wages to effectively stagnate in return for job guarantees.

But much of the change took place below anybody's radar at companies like Pickhan Heavy Fabrication. You probably have never heard of Pickhan, based in the small city of Siegen, in a hilly region of western Germany. But if you have been to the Museum of Modern Art in New York or the Gap headquarters in San Francisco, you have probably seen its products. When I visited Pickhan in 2007, its main factory looked like little more than an oversized welding workshop. The owner, Friedhelm Pickhan, did not come across as your typical CEO. He was a compact man with a voice like sandpaper, who smoked Marlboro Lights, which he stubbed out when they were halfway done, putting the rest back in the package to enjoy later. Pickhan was what Germans call a *Handwerker*. They mean it as a compliment.

Pickhan's most famous customer was Richard Serra, the American sculptor. Pickhan fabricated Serra's huge sculptures of undulating steel, in part because no American company was capable of doing the work to his standards. Works that Pickhan made for Serra are found in leading museums, prominent public spaces, and corporate headquarters around the world. Pickhan was, moreover, one of the few companies anywhere near capable of shaping huge pieces of steel with great precision into irregular shapes.

Pickhan took a huge risk when it accepted its first commission from Serra in 1997. As Friedhelm Pickhan told me the story in 2007,[5] the artist, who had heard about the shop from his German art dealer, faxed over a few curved lines drawn with a thick pencil on a sheet of paper. He asked Pickhan if he could make it. Pickhan did not know much about art or have much use for artists, but he had just bought a big new machine and needed work to do on it. He said he would try. Pickhan had to knock out a wall of the factory building to accommodate the huge sheets of steel needed to construct Serra's sculpture. Centimeter by centimeter, Pickhan and his workers fed the sheets through a press that folded them into the precise, subtle shapes that the artist wanted. It was part heavy industry, part origami.

Serra entitled that first work *Pickhan's Progress*. It later went on view at the Museum of Contemporary Art in Los Angeles. Pickhan made dozens of Serra sculptures in the years that followed. Moreover, the association with Serra was the jumping off point for a huge expansion of Pickhan's business. In the years after that first assignment from Serra, the company built a thriving business supplying shipbuilders and makers of offshore oil drilling equipment and other customers who require big pieces of steel in precise, tailored shapes.

Companies like Pickhan, which Friedhelm Pickhan sold in 2009[6], are arguably the soul of the German economy. Almost any city of any size has at least one or two of these *Mittelstand* companies, if not more. They are often not start-ups in the traditional sense of the word. Most have been around for decades, if not centuries. Pickhan began as a maker of metal rims for wagon wheels—a product it was still making in the 1950s. It is not at all unusual for their managers to be third- or fourth-generation descendants of the founders. These managers are much more likely to have attended engineering school than an MBA program. They like to make things.

An American banker friend of mine tells a story that illustrates the mentality. Some years back, he was involved in setting up a private equity fund for one of the world's largest investment banks. My friend learned of a German machinery company that might be for sale and flew over from London to visit the owner. As my friend and his colleagues were in the middle of describing how their multibillion-dollar fund could make the owner very, very rich, a man in greasy blue coveralls burst into the office. He was holding a piece of equipment that was causing a problem. Ignoring the bankers in their expensive suits, the company owner took the piece of equipment—a gear of some sort that dripped oil on the conference table—and spent ten minutes turning it over in his hands and explaining to the man in coveralls how to solve the problem.

At one level, my friend was appalled that the owner would rudely interrupt a meeting with the bankers from London whose briefcases were figuratively bulging with money. But at another level he was impressed. The owner was more focused on his products than on deal making, more focused on building things than accumulating wealth. My friend later started his own private equity company that invests in medium-sized companies in Germany. He has done pretty well.

The flip side of this mentality is that German business people can be naïve or negligent on matters involving finance and marketing. They are risk averse and, at least on the surface, tradition bound. When they borrow money at all, the credit usually comes from a local savings bank. They recoil at the idea of a stock listing. A few have begun issuing corporate bonds, but their use of capital markets for financing is still far behind companies in the United States.

What sets these companies apart is their ability to identify a market niche, usually one where price is a secondary competitive factor, and use superior design and engineering to dominate the market globally. While conservative, they are capable of daring when confronted with the right opportunity, as illustrated by Pickhan's willingness to knock a hole in the workshop wall to accommodate Serra. Though initially slow to exploit the Internet or make use of information technology, German companies soon realized its potential as a tool for managing the factory and conducting transactions far outside their traditional markets. As new markets opened up in Asia and Latin America, they learned to operate like multinationals even if they only had 30 employees.

German companies have learned these skills because they had no choice. The domestic market has always been relatively small, in contrast to the United States, the largest market in the world. But since the emergence of China, American companies have also learned the perils of relying too much on products aimed at a mass market and dependent on the domestic economy. In a globalized economy, such products are vulnerable to a foreign competitor who can offer comparable quality at a lower price.

It is telling that Serra went all the way to Germany to find someone who could build his sculptures. When I reached Serra by phone several years ago, the artist told me that his previous fabricator was a company in Baltimore that had closed down. The decline of American industry is not news, of course. And the German economy has long been more dependent on industry than the United States. In 1980, manufacturing value added—in other words, the value of manufactured goods minus the preexisting value of the raw materials and components that came from outside the country—was 30 percent of GDP in Germany and 22 percent in the United States, according to World Bank data. By 2010, the corresponding figures had fallen to

21 percent in Germany and 13 percent in the United States.[7] So that is a 30 percent decline in German manufacturing as a proportion of the economy, and a 41 percent decline in the United States. Both countries suffered a decline in industry, but the slump was much greater in the United States. And the decline in German industry may be over-stated. German exports accounted for half of GDP in 2012, up from 30 percent in 2000.[8] The increase suggests that the decline in production of goods has been more than offset by an increase in industry-related services, like designing and supervising construction of new steel plants in China. And manufacturing jobs in German have been fairly stable in the last decade, at about 7.2 million. In the United States, factory jobs fell from 14.6 million in 2004 to 12 million in 2011, though there are signs of a revival.[9]

The German renaissance occurred even though German companies face obstacles that their American peers do not. For the most part U.S. companies do not have to contend with strong unions, or labor laws that, even after recent reforms in Germany, make it difficult and costly to lay off workers. In Germany, employees often sue if they are fired for poor performance. There is a whole separate court system to handle their complaints.[10] Companies often find it easier and cheaper simply to offer the worker money to leave. Large job cuts in response to a slump in business are also difficult. Employers must typically negotiate a "social plan" with the workers council, which attempts to ease the trauma of job loss by offering severance payments and letting go the workers most able to absorb the shock. That means younger people without families are usually the first to lose their jobs. Proponents of the German system, a group that includes most German voters, believe their system to be more humane. But it is certainly more costly and inconvenient for employers.

Companies in the United States also have access to a much larger and more active capital market, making it easier for them to raise money by issuing stocks or bonds. In Germany, and most of Europe, banks are still the predominant source of financing for all but the largest companies. For an advanced country, Germany ranks poorly in measures of access to financing. In the World Economic Forum's 2013–2014 competitiveness rankings, Germany placed sixth overall, one place ahead of the United States. But Germany was in thirty-fourth place in availability of financing from equity markets, and thirty-third in access to venture capital, just behind Bolivia.[11]

Germany is a less enthusiastically digital society than the United States. Its record as an incubator of new information technology is mixed. SAP, a leading maker of the enterprise software that companies use to manage operations like transport, finance, or personnel, is a German company. MP3, the encoding standard that made music downloads possible, was developed by a unit of the Fraunhofer Institute—though commercial exploitation mostly happened elsewhere. But Silicon Valley remains the epicenter of global technology innovation. Attempts to create similar clusters of digital creativity in places like Munich have not had much impact— although Berlin is beginning to show promise. Germans have played a key role in the evolution of the Internet, but they often did so in California, not Munich. Andreas von Bechtolsheim, a German who cofounded Sun Microsystems and was an early investor in Google, is one example of an entrepreneur who realized his full potential only by going to America. The World Economic Forum gives Germany middling scores in measures of its ability to exploit information technology. In 2013, it ranked thirteenth in "availability of advanced technologies," for example.[12] (The United States was sixth.)[13] The Neuer Markt, the Frankfurt Stock Exchange's answer to NASDAQ, proved to be a massive destroyer of shareholder wealth and was closed in 2003.

To sum up, U.S. companies have better access to financing, more compliant labor, and an edge in technology, not to mention cheaper energy and more abundant natural resources. So if American companies have so many natural advantages, why are German companies leading in so many foreign markets? What is it about German traditions, mentality, education, and business practices that make the German economy what it is? What methods can companies in other countries adopt to become as successful?

To answer those questions, we will get to know a number of German managers and the companies they run. They range in size from Bollin Armaturenfabrik in Frankfurt, with just 30 workers, to automaker BMW in Munich, with more than 100,000. I chose these companies because they illustrate the principles that distinguish the German way of doing business, they make interesting products, and I found the managers likeable and engaging and hoped that readers would, too. *Mittelstand* managers have been among the most rewarding interview subjects I have encountered during my two decades of writing about business in Germany. They are, more often than not, what the Germans call *bodenständig*—someone who stands solidly on the *Boden*, the ground. They tend to be frank and unassuming. You ask a question, and they answer it. How often I have negotiated for months to interview the chief executive of a big publicly traded multinational, only to have him steadfastly repeat boilerplate phrases from the company's annual report, surrounded by media advisers whose job is to make sure he says nothing that might accidently upset the stock market. (One public relations person I know later admitted to me that she used a system of secret hand signals to restrain her boss, something of a loose cannon, should he stray off message.)

Mittelstand managers have no such compunctions. They are refreshingly straightforward and unafraid to say what is on their minds. They identify strongly with the companies they run, and their passion is infectious. The overused phrase "It's in their DNA" is apt in this case—often their family histories are inseparable from the history of their companies. They grew up hearing about the family business at the dinner table, absorbing lessons that no university could teach. My affinity for these managers may have something to do with my own family history. My maternal grandfather, Leonard Kruysman, belonged to the American industrial Mittelstand when one still existed. He was the founder of a company that made expandable envelopes used primarily by law firms, and he coined the term used to describe the product, Redweld. His factory was in a building on Spring Street in downtown Manhattan, in a neighborhood where most of the industrial space has since been converted to luxury residential lofts. As a teenager I spent a summer riding shotgun in the company van with a driver named Rocco, hauling boxes of Redwelds up freight elevators to swanky Manhattan law firms. My grandfather paid me $25 a week, plus room and board. So maybe I have a little Mittelstand DNA in me. The aim of this book is to impart a little Mittelstand DNA to the reader, as well. But first, a short history lesson.

A Brief History of Made in Germany

The British officials who coined the phrase "Made in Germany" intended it as an insult. In 1887, alarmed at an influx of low-priced German products, the British government required goods imported from Germany to be labeled as such. Back then, Germany was to Britain something like China is to Europe or the United States today. It was an aggressive emerging economy with a large store of cheap labor and ambitions to become an economic superpower. But Britain's attempt to shield domestic companies from competition backfired. Made in Germany became a synonym for quality.[1] The story of how Germany succeeded within a few decades still tells us something about the German mindset and tradition.

The Industrial Revolution came late to Germany, but transformed the economy with astonishing speed once it did. Well into the nineteenth century, Germany had been politically fragmented and economically backward. Serfdom, the system that tied farmers to landowners and gave the nobility far-reaching powers over farmers' lives, persisted until the beginning of the 1800s in some regions, including Prussia, the most powerful German state. Centuries after the end of feudalism in Britain, a significant percentage of the German population was locked into an agrarian economy, miserably poor and uneducated, unavailable as factory labor much less as a source of entrepreneurship.

What we know as Germany today did not yet exist. The German-speaking world then revolved around two empires, Prussia and Austria, German-dominated but with a polyglot citizenry, with a patchwork of fiefdoms sandwiched in-between. Goods traversing the region were subject to duties each time they crossed the borders of independent states like Württemberg or Bavaria. The barriers suppressed trade, and were deep enough that some of their legacy persists today. While high German is the language of the educated classes and business interchange, many regional dialects survive and are still the everyday means of communication in places like Bavaria or the area bordering Denmark. These are more than just regional accents. Some dialects are so impenetrable that, when a native is interviewed on German television, broadcasters superimpose subtitles so that viewers elsewhere in the country can understand. These linguistic demarcations are, in a sense, the ghosts of ancient economic and political barriers.

Reform of the German system began after the French Revolution at the end of the eighteenth century. Germany's own democratic movement during that period would eventually fail, but the ruling class was well aware of the unrest brewing among the broad German population. Living standards for the poor, already abysmal, were declining at the same time that expectations were rising, as mechanized farming displaced farm laborers and citizens learned of the democratic change taking place elsewhere. Fear of French-style chaos served as an impetus for the ruling class and bourgeoisie to reluctantly accept limited change, including liberation of the serfs and, beginning in 1818 in Prussia, the creation of the *Zollverein*, a customs union. The free trade zone expanded in the years to come, allowing easier movement of goods within the German-speaking world.

The creation of Germany as a coherent political entity in the 1870s was largely the product of the machinations of Otto von Bismarck, the chancellor of Prussia. Ruthless and pragmatic, Bismarck was clever enough to see that concessions to the popular will were necessary to preserve the power and privileges of the nobility. He managed to thwart true democratic rule, yet introduced changes such as health insurance that improved the lot of ordinary workers. In 1883, 130 years before Obamacare, German workers received free medical treatment and medicines, as well as sick pay when they were unable to work for longer periods. Thanks in part to Bismarck, Germans today take it for granted that the government will pay for health care and education and protect them from the harsher effects of free-market capitalism.

Intertwined with political change was the unstoppable advance of a new technology, the railroad. The advent of rail travel was significant not only because it speeded the transport of goods and people but also because it created huge demand for rails and locomotives. The first railroad equipment was imported from Britain, but Germans quickly learned to produce their own. By 1853, domestic companies accounted for 94 percent of German locomotive production.[2] The German steel and machinery industries were born.

Why did Germany so readily develop its own manufacturing base for railroads when other countries like Italy did not? The presence of coal, particularly in the Ruhr Valley, offers a partial explanation. But Germany—by which I mean the region we now call Germany—also seemed to have an abundant supply of what today we would call entrepreneurs: restless, ambitious souls who single-mindedly pursued new markets and technologies. The militarism of Prussian society also played a role, creating a demand for military engineers and a route for young men of common birth to acquire training. The poverty and overpopulation of the German-speaking regions also provided a powerful impetus for people to seek routes to better lives. Huge numbers immigrated to America, but some remained and built companies whose names are still to be found on corporate logos. Alfred Krupp springs to mind. Krupp was just 14 when his father's death in 1826 left him with much of the responsibility for the family iron works.[3] The young man recognized the opportunity offered by the advent of railroads, and began producing axles and other parts for locomotives. The company's breakthrough came in 1852 and 1853 when Alfred Krupp developed a seamless rail wheel, which could operate at faster speeds without disintegrating. The firm Krupp began producing ingots for artillery pieces in 1847. Not content with being merely a subcontractor, producing blanks to be finished by someone else,

Alfred Krupp developed his own cannons, which he began selling to the Prussian military in 1859. The name Krupp would soon become synonymous with German military aggression.

To a great extent, Alfred Krupp set the template for hundreds of German business leaders to follow. He was not a founder in the strict sense of the word. He took over a family business, but transformed it into something far grander than the company he inherited. Many of the companies we will meet later in this book adhere to this pattern. Krupp was an innovator, who did not merely exploit the inventions of others but built sales by developing new products that were superior to the competition and owned exclusively by the company. Today we take it for granted that companies conduct their own research and development, but this was a novelty in that era. Alfred Krupp recognized that the most sophisticated products generated the most profit. Nowadays we would say that Krupp aimed for the premium market, the top of the value chain. He was not satisfied merely to make tubes that another company would upgrade into field pieces. The way to make money was to deliver the most technically challenging part of the process, to do things that competitors could not.

But the Krupp company in the nineteenth century also aimed for the bottom of the value chain. Alfred Krupp wanted to control every step of production, even the mines that produced iron ore. The Krupp firm also maintained its own international sales force. Economic historian Richard Tilly has argued that this vertical integration, as we would call it today, gave Krupp and other German companies an advantage over British competitors, which operated under a mercantile system steered by the government and used as an instrument of foreign policy. The German companies were closer to their customers and suppliers, and had better information about what was happening in the market.[4] That level of vertical integration is pursued by only a few companies today, but there are occasional exceptions. In 2013, when BMW began mass producing an electric car with a body made largely of lightweight carbon fiber, it decided to produce the raw material itself in Washington State by way of a joint venture with SGL Carbon. No existing supplier could produce what BMW needed. And the practice of building and maintaining a foreign sales and service organization remains widespread, even for smaller German companies.

Werner von Siemens is another name that looms large in German economic history. Born in 1816, a few years after Krupp, Siemens was one of 14 children of a poor tenant farmer in a small town near Hanover. He is an example of the human potential that was set free after cracks appeared in the class system, and the Industrial Revolution offered a path of upward mobility for young men of talent and ambition. (Siemens earned the aristocratic "von" much later.) Unable to afford a higher education, Siemens joined the Prussian Army as a way to learn engineering. While still serving, he invented a so-called pointer telegraph that did not require knowledge of Morse code to use. It became the basis for the company he formed with a partner in 1847, Siemens & Halske.[5] After winning an order to build the first telegraph line between Berlin and Frankfurt, Siemens moved abroad in search of new business, building telegraph lines in Russia and Britain. Later he played an important role in the development and commercialization of large-scale electrical power generation, which remains a major part of the modern Siemens empire.

Like Krupp, Werner von Siemens established enduring precedents for German business leaders to follow. He was an engineer first, albeit with a keen nose for business, who seemed to take intrinsic pleasure in inventing things. Siemens once wrote to his brother Carl: "For me the business is only secondarily important as a source of wealth: I see it rather as a realm that I have founded and that I would like to pass on undiminished to my descendants so that they can continue to operate within it."[6] That statement could serve as a motto for countless German entrepreneurs today, for whom the act of making something is more satisfying than the accumulation of money. Werner von Siemens was also an early example of a German entrepreneur who moved fearlessly into foreign markets like Russia or the Middle East, which offered much greater potential than the German market alone.

Alongside the industrial giants were thousands of small companies that filled the niches in which the big companies had no interest. According to historian Paul Erker, "practically every mid-sized city in Germany had small family-owned machinery factories."[7] These were the forerunners of the *Mittelstand*, the smaller, highly focused companies that more than any other sector drive the German economy today. Glasbau Hahn, a maker of museum display cases that we will meet later in this book, already existed in this era.

One reason that Krupp and Siemens and many other German entrepreneurs were innovative and international was because they had no choice if they were to compete abroad with England. Germany had limited natural resources. Germany's navy was far inferior to Britain's, and its access to the open ocean was constrained. Germany had only a modest foreign empire compared to Britain. As we have seen, Germany was not even a unified country until the Industrial Revolution was well under way.

Despite, or perhaps because of, these drawbacks, by the end of the nineteenth century Germany had by far the more inventive, technology-oriented economy. German inventors registered 11 times as many patents between 1885 and 1890 as Britain. Building on the Prussian educational system, which was designed to provide technical expertise for the army, German colleges trained 3,000 engineers a year by the turn of the century, eight times as many as Britain. The number of university-educated managers in Germany was at a level that Britain did not reach for another half century.[8] German managers served apprenticeships in British factories to learn their methods and technology, and imported British experts to work in German factories.[9] They also traveled to the United States to learn mass-production methods.[10] This emphasis on technical training and education, on *Ausbildung*, remains a key feature of the German economy. And ambitious young German men and women still spend time traveling and working abroad to learn about other cultures and ways of doing things.

In the second half of the nineteenth century, German exports grew faster than Britain's, threatening English pre-eminence in the global economy. The British were well aware of the threat, convening a Royal commission to study the issue, which in 1887 issued the edict requiring the Made in Germany label. However, more than feeble protectionism was required to stop the German industrial advance. By 1913, on the eve of World War I, Germany accounted for 12.3 percent of world trade, just behind Britain with 14.2 percent, and ahead of the United States with 11 percent.[11] Sales abroad accounted for more than one-third of German national income. The Krupp company employed 64,000 workers in 1907, as many as its modern incarnation, ThyssenKrupp, had in Germany in 2012.[12] Germany had become unequivocally an export nation, which makes the decisions of German political and military leaders during those years seem, in retrospect, all the more foolish and inexplicable, to say nothing of tragic.

It would be misleading, however, to portray the nineteenth century as a steady advance toward prosperity that was derailed only by the hubris of Kaiser Wilhelm and his generals. It was a volatile period, marked by frequent military conflict and recurrent economic crises. For most ordinary people, life was difficult at best and often miserable. Working conditions were abysmal, the pay was barely enough to survive, and getting enough to eat was an overwhelming concern. German managers could be as reckless as they were innovative. The Krupp company was continually beset by financial crises due to overexpansion and miscalculation by Alfred Krupp and his successors. As Krupp, Siemens, and other companies like Bayer grew into giant enterprises, they sought to protect themselves from the competition that, decades earlier, they had once personified. They coined a new term, the *Interessengemeinschaft*, or IG. Literally, it meant a community of interests; in practice it was a cartel. Toward the end of the 1880s, many large companies succumbed to the temptation to join forces, with government blessing, to shield themselves from domestic competition. The chemical industry was the most prominent example. Two cartels controlled 95 percent of German production of dye, which native chemists had learned to synthesize from chemicals rather than natural substances, and which was then the most important chemical product. Worldwide, they controlled 80 percent of production.[13] Later, the chemical industry cartel known as IG Farben— *Farben* being the German word for dye—would become notorious for its role in the Holocaust, for its use of slave labor, and as supplier of Zyklon B, the insecticide gas used to kill Jews.

All of that lay in the future. On the eve of World War I, German leaders could look back on a century in which they had gone from a postfeudal agrarian economy to a global commercial power. German companies had established traditions that would endure another century and beyond. They were innovative and global. Yet they retained a provincial preference for family ownership. Though inherently cautious, they were capable of boldness, even recklessness, when the rewards—or threats—seemed great enough. They placed considerable emphasis on education. They were not immune to the temptations of oligarchy.

The German decision to attack France by way of Belgium in 1914 set in motion events of such monumental human tragedy that it seems almost petty to focus on the economic consequences. Nevertheless, for the purposes of understanding the modern German economy, let us briefly survey the effect that the two world wars had on German business.

They were, needless to say, disastrous. The Kaiser and his generals grossly underestimated the cost and duration of the war. The army drained 13 million Germans from the workforce, 20 percent of the population, of which 3 million were killed.[14] The domestic economy was converted almost entirely to war production, creating great privation for the German population. While World War I did not bring the kind of property destruction on German soil that would mark the next war, the post-Armistice effects were still enormous. German companies were cut off from the international markets they had so skillfully exploited. Germany's international patents were nullified, allowing competitors to steal German technology. American companies could now make Aspirin, for example, robbing Bayer of its monopoly. German wealth abroad was seized.

The political and economic turmoil that characterized the years between the wars was hardly favorable for business, which needs stability and predictability. But some clever people profited from the hyperinflation of 1923 in ways that would have a lasting effect on the German industrial scene. Günther Quandt was one example.[15] The wealthy scion of a textile manufacturer who produced uniforms during World War I, he bought battery maker Varta using devalued Reichsmarks, helping to create the basis for the fortune his son, Herbert, would later use to acquire Bayerische Motoren Werke. His ancestors still control BMW. Another development is worth mentioning. In an effort to calm worker unrest, German companies introduced the concept of *Mitbestimmung*—the practice of giving workers councils a voice in company management. This was the same strategy used by Bismarck in the previous century. The business and government elite made concessions on issues of great everyday importance to the working class in the interest of maintaining overall control.

The Nazi period was not, as many people inside and outside Germany believe to this day, a period of economic prosperity and technological advance, albeit one purchased by a pact with the Hitler devil. After the hyperinflation of the 1920s and the deflation and government austerity that preceded the Nazi period, Germany was poised in any case for a recovery. German technical superiority was overrated, a result of the Nazi *Wunderwaffen* propaganda that even outsiders subconsciously accepted. The feared Wehrmacht depended on horses for transport. British and American jet turbine technology was more advanced, even if Germany— desperate to fight allied bombing—deployed jet aircraft sooner. German scientists were far behind the British and Americans in development and deployment of radar.[16]

The Aryanization of German industry, carried out with the complicity of German business, deprived the German economy of some of its savviest bankers and entrepreneurs. The Frankfurt banking industry had largely been created by Mayer Amschel Rothschild and his descendants, whose services to Hessian nobility in the eighteenth century freed the city's Jewish community from the ghetto. The expulsion of Jews from Deutsche Bank, Commerzbank, and other lenders during the Nazi period deprived those institutions of a crucial source of expertise. Observing the sorry state of German banks and capital markets today, one is tempted to wonder whether they ever recovered. At this writing, Dresdner Bank has disappeared, Commerzbank is under government control, and Deutsche Bank is struggling to retain its stature among global investment banks. In comparison with the United States, German capital markets remain underdeveloped. In America, roughly two-thirds of business financing comes from capital markets, and one-third from banks. In Germany, the proportion is reversed. Germans remain averse to raising money on the stock market. Major companies such as Bosch, one of the world's largest suppliers of auto electronics, remain privately held. This may be an advantage in the German context, however. The German economy produces capital goods, big-ticket items that are highly susceptible to economic ups and downs. Without pressure from stockholders to produce ever-growing quarterly earnings, German companies are able to plan for the long term. They require competent, prudent managers to take advantage of that freedom, however.

Just as Nazi industrial prowess was exaggerated, so was the effect of Allied bombing on German industry. A U.S. Air Force survey in 1944 found that bombing had damaged only 6.5 percent of all machines, and of those, only 10 percent were completely unusable.[17] British night bombing targeted worker housing blocks, based on the cold-blooded and accurate calculation that skilled labor was easier to destroy and harder to replace than machines.

While the loss of manpower was huge, West Germany benefited during the postwar years from an influx of skilled Germans expelled from Czechoslovakia, Poland, and other areas of Eastern Europe that had been part of historical Prussia or had large German populations. One of them was Herbert Kannegiesser, a refugee from a region now part of Poland who had studied engineering and worked in the aircraft industry. Kannegiesser landed in Vlotho, a small town in northwestern Germany that was a center of the country's textile industry. Recognizing that the manufacturers needed equipment, Kannegiesser and his wife, Irma, began producing machines to press newly manufactured shirts. It was a workshop operation at first, with just the Kannegiessers and two employees, but grew quickly. The garment industry would eventually desert Germany and Europe for Asia or other places where labor was cheap. But Kannegiesser, focused on the segment of the business that required the most technological expertise, remained and became an international supplier with a network of factories and some 300 million euros a year in sales. We will meet Herbert Kannegiesser's son, Martin, later in this book.

Germany in 1945 was traumatized, starving, and chaotic. Its cities were in ruins. But as bad as things seemed for most German citizens, the conditions for business were, in the words of historian Erker, "not so bad."[18]

2

Revival

There is a famous photograph of Reinhard Mohn, scion of the family that owned the book publisher C. Bertelsmann, taken in 1947. Mohn was a veteran of the Afrika Korps who had returned the year before from an American prisoner of war (POW) camp. The photo shows him addressing the workforce at Bertelsmann in the city of Gütersloh, in northwestern Germany. Mohn is wearing a heavy woolen military-style coat that looks too big for his thin frame, and stands behind a lectern that appears to have been hammered together from plywood. A lamp, little more than a bare light bulb, hangs from a plank nailed to the lectern, illuminating Mohn's face. Some employees stand behind him, and in their faces you can see something of the grimness of German life in those first years after the war. There was not enough food or fuel, and many sons and fathers were still in Russian prison camps, if not missing or dead. The people's faces are serious. The atrocities and aggression of the Nazis had left Germany drenched in shame. Were the employees hungry, fearful, traumatized? It is impossible to say, but no one is smiling. Mohn's face, however, is resolute, almost bright. His cheeks are hollow, but he seems to be looking toward the future with optimism.

Mohn could not have anticipated then, of course, that six decades later Bertelsmann would become a global media company, the largest publisher of English-language books via its Random House subsidiary, and the largest television broadcaster in Europe, by way of the RTL family of stations. Bertelsmann would employ more than 100,000 people around the world. A Bertelsmann subsidiary would create *American Idol* and its many clones around the world—for better or worse.

But Mohn appears in that old photo to have recognized, at some level, the opportunities that lay ahead for business people with drive. Despite all the material and spiritual privations of the postwar years, the German economy was wide open. IG Farben and the other monopolies had been broken apart by the Allies. (The American military took over IG Farben's stately, beige brick office complex in Frankfurt's West End and used it as a headquarters; today it is a university campus.) The last privileges of the nobility were abolished, so that obstacles based on class and birth were lower than in Germany's eternal economic rival, Britain. The German population was eager, even desperate, for a better life and anxious to acquire material goods. Most markets lacked a dominant player, or any player at all. Beyond the ruins lay opportunity.

The destruction of German infrastructure and industry was not as complete as photos of rubble-strewn cities suggest. Someone visiting Gütersloh right after the war would have found what appeared to be a grim tableau. A British bombing raid in March 1945 had destroyed most of the buildings that Bertelsmann used for production, and the main office headquarters burned to the ground after an incendiary bomb landed nearby. But there was no loss of life from the raid. Of 17 printing machines, only one was completely destroyed.

Mohn illustrates a pattern that would repeat itself countless times in postwar Germany. Like Krupp more than a century earlier, Mohn was not a founder in the strict sense. Bertelsmann was already a sizeable publisher by the standards of the time. Despite its history as a printer of Bibles, Bertelsmann had thrived by accommodating itself to the Nazi regime, becoming the largest supplier of books for the Wehrmacht, pulp novels designed to support the soldiers' morale. Some of its material was anti-Semitic.[1] Even at its peak in the war years, Bertelsmann was a relatively small company, with about 400 workers, and only 150 at war's end. But it proved enough for an ambitious and creative manager to build something much larger.

Mohn had many counterparts in the years right after the war—young men who took over small family businesses and built them into much larger companies that bore only a faint resemblance to what they had inherited. Another example was Ferdinand "Ferry" Porsche, who assumed control of the family engineering and design shop in a Stuttgart suburb and began making sports cars. Berthold Leibinger began work in 1950 as an apprentice at a small machinery company called Trumpf in a suburb of Stuttgart, not far from where Porsche's headquarters is located today. Though he was not a member of the Trumpf family, Leibinger was energetic and creative, and something of a surrogate son to the company owner. Within a few years he had patented numerous new methods of cutting sheet metal, creating the basis for what became a multinational company with billions of euros in sales. As he recalled later, any company in the western zone of Germany that could manage to produce something useful found a ready market. "Indeed, not to have been economically successful during those first years would have been quite a feat," Leibinger wrote.[2]

Younger German managers were highly motivated. After the catastrophic defeats of the two world wars, it was clear to any rational person that Germany could not assert itself in the world by means of military force. To young men like Leibinger, industry provided both a channel for their ambition and a way to regain respect after the shame of the Holocaust. "We were driven by the need to show that there was another Germany, a Germany of understanding and openness," Leibinger recalled years later, at age 82.[3]

The younger managers were often less tainted by Nazi associations than their elders. Leibinger was 14 when the war ended. After being captured in North Africa, Mohn had spent most of the war at a POW camp in Kansas, where he learned English and something of American business practices.[4] With the younger Mohn in charge, rather than his ill and politically tainted father, Bertelsmann was able to win printing contracts from the British forces that occupied a sector of West Germany.

For many of these young people, one lesson of the war was that America had prevailed because it was a dynamic, creative entrepreneurial society, one they should emulate. Many made it a point to travel there. Berthold Leibinger went to Ohio, where he managed to get a job at the Cincinnati Milling Co., then the largest maker of machine tools in the world. Decades later, Trumpf would have sales in the billions and dwarf what remained of Cincinnati Milling.

There were plenty of start-up companies in those postwar years as well. We have already heard about Herbert Kannegiesser. Another example was Max Grundig, who used his knowledge of radios to build what for a time was one of the world's largest consumer electronics companies. Most German consumers knew only the primitive *Volksempfänger*, a radio designed to receive Nazi propaganda. There were no televisions. Grundig stepped into an almost completely empty market. Leo Kirch was another who took advantage of a poorly served market, the one for entertainment. Much of Germany's cultural elite, stars like Marlene Dietrich or authors like Thomas Mann, had been driven into exile by the Nazis. Those who stayed behind and kept working inevitably became part of the Nazi propaganda machine, and were discredited. Leo Kirch, recognizing the hunger for diversion, drove to Italy in a Volkswagen Beetle, where he acquired the German distribution rights to Federico Fellini's sad tale of a circus strongman, *La Strada*. In the years to come, Kirch parlayed the proceeds into a television and film-rights empire. But while there were certainly examples of successful start-ups, much of the economic growth to follow was built on foundations laid decades earlier.

Germany's traditional industrial powers revived quickly. As the Cold War developed and it became clear that the division of Germany was permanent, the Western Allies eased restrictions on large companies stained by their role in the Nazi war machine. Plans to convert Germany to an agrarian economy proved wholly impractical—there was not nearly enough land to feed the population—and Germany's help was needed to meet the Soviet threat. Krupp reemerged as a power in the steel industry, despite its involvement in war crimes. Krupp had used forced laborers during the war who were held under abysmal conditions, and Alfried Krupp, a descendent of the man who had built the company into a crucial component of the German war machine, served time in prison for war crimes. The Krupp family soon lost control of the company, however.[5] Even today, at least two-thirds of the blue-chip DAX 30 stock index has prewar roots, albeit sometimes with different names. They represent many of the best-known companies in German industry today, including Siemens, Daimler, and BMW.

Not that German companies had it easy. While Allied bombing had not been very effective at putting machinery out of action, it had destroyed bridges, rail lines, and other transportation links. The French and the Soviets confiscated machinery and installed it in their own factories. (In 2006, I was surprised to see prewar German rolling machines in use at an aluminum factory in Hungary. Managers told me the machines, which had been upgraded with modern computer control technology, still worked beautifully.) Bertelsmann had machines with which to print books, but its customers could not get to the bookstores to buy them. The distribution problem became so acute that in 1949 Bertelsmann nearly went out of business. It was in such situations that German companies were able to draw on the tradition of innovation established by the likes of Werner von Siemens. Bertelsmann invented the *Lesering*, the Reader's Circle, a form of book club that delivered the latest titles to the homes of customers. After a year, the Lesering had 100,000 customers. In four years it had a million.[6] Bertelsmann owes its later existence as a global multinational to this simple, profitable idea.

Almost every manager of a family company can tell stories about the desperation of the postwar years, and how he or she was forced to find creative ways to survive. Glasbau Hahn, a glassmaker in Frankfurt, made etched souvenir glass coasters that it peddled to American GIs—about the only group with disposable income right after the war. That so many family companies still exist is a reflection of the power of familial duty and tradition. Those that survived learned lessons and established traditions that would influence their business conduct in the decades to come.

By the beginning of the 1950s, a semblance of prosperity returned, helped by a currency reform that substituted new deutsche marks for the old reichsmarks. From 1951 to 1961, the German economy grew by an average of 8 percent per year.[7] "The new money worked wonders," Berthold Leibinger wrote. "We already had a cozy feeling that prosperity and luxury were possible even in Germany, and that we were allowed to strive after them."[8]

3

The Seeds of Complacency

The economics minister in the postwar years, Ludwig Erhard, embraced a new idea, coined by the economist Alfred Müller-Armack, that proved to have enduring force: the social-market economy. It was a riposte to Soviet-style socialism, of which the promise of economic equality was appealing to some Germans at the time, suffering as they were from lack of basic food and shelter. Erhard, a conservative who later became chancellor and is considered one of the founding fathers of postwar West German democracy, struck a social contract that endures to this day. The state would protect German citizens from the harsher consequences of capitalism, while giving German entrepreneurs enough freedom to compete in the foreign markets that were so essential to their success. Lacking Otto von Bismarck's cynical intent, it was a variation on the health insurance and pensions that the Iron Chancellor had used in the previous century to contain democratic unrest. This time, the idea was to undercut any possible appeal of the model taking shape in East Germany. The disadvantage of the system, however, was that it ran the risk of muting signals from the market and encouraging complacency.

As the German system evolved in the coming decades, it came to offer a long catalogue of protections and entitlements. They included generous pensions for retired workers and nearly open-ended unemployment benefits that covered much of a jobless worker's lost wages. The government-sanctioned health insurance program allowed people to choose their own doctors and did not require copayments beyond the basic premium. Workers were even entitled to periodic stays in health spas to recover from injuries or merely the stress of daily life.

German law guaranteed the influence of labor unions and gave workers a voice in company management that would be unthinkable in the United States. A law enacted in 1976 granted employees in larger enterprises the right to half the seats on company supervisory boards. The chairman, appointed by owners, had the power to break ties, giving shareholders a one-vote majority. Wages were negotiated on a regional and industry-wide basis. That meant, for example, that the union representing metal and auto industry workers in the state of Baden-Württemberg would negotiate with the corresponding employers' association on behalf of the whole sector. The agreement would apply to big companies like Daimler, based in the state capital of Stuttgart, as well as the small and mid-size companies that supplied components for Mercedes cars. Agreements in one region were generally copied in others, so that in effect there was nationwide wage setting. The system saved companies from having to conduct their own negotiations, but took little account of the varying circumstances of individual firms. A small auto parts supplier had to pay its workers wages comparable to those at Daimler.

For a long time, this system worked fairly well and was supported by both major political parties, the center-left Social Democrats and the center-right Christian Democrats. Despite the constraints placed on management, the system offered advantages from the point of view of companies. Reaching consensus on company supervisory boards could be laborious, but once achieved meant that workers had a stake in the decision-making. They were more motivated to support management goals and strategy. Unlike France or Italy, Germany was rarely hit by crippling work stoppages. When German unions wanted to remind management of their clout, they used limited warning strikes. The number of workdays lost to labor strife was low compared to other European countries.

Many features of the German system were also cozy for business. Most of the banking system was in quasi-public hands. At the local level, savings banks known as *Sparkassen* dominated consumer and small-business lending. Local politicians typically sat on the boards of Sparkassen and were prone to use them to exert influence over the local economy and win votes. The Sparkassen, usually in league with state governments, owned regional lenders known as *Landesbanken*. The Landesbanken enjoyed government guarantees, which allowed them to raise money on capital markets more cheaply than commercial banks and gave them a competitive advantage. They also ensured that businesses could borrow at rates that were effectively subsidized by the government.

The system was comfortable for those who benefited, but it was expensive. To some historians, the *Wirtschaftswunder*[1] ended in 1973 when the Arab oil crisis drove up oil prices and led to a sharp slowdown. In 1975, gross domestic product (GDP) fell 0.9 percent, only the second year of declining output since 1950. Certainly, economic growth after the 1970s never again reached the velocity of the 1950s and 1960s, when GDP routinely rose more than 5 percent and rarely much less than 3 percent. After 1975, annual growth never again topped 5 percent. But it sometimes came close and rarely fell below 2 percent.[2] Living standards continued to rise, albeit at a slower pace. There was little financial or political pressure to change the system.

The German economy began to show severe strain following the fall of the Berlin Wall and the reunification of West and East Germany. Under the illusion that East Germany could quickly be brought up to West German living standards, unions and employers set wages in the east at 62 percent of the western level.[3] West German unions claimed they were acting in solidarity with their East German comrades, but they also had an interest in preventing the creation of a low-wage zone within their own country.

It swiftly became clear that East German industry was obsolete and inefficient, often producing goods for which there was little or no real market. During a trip to Saxony early in the 2000s, my local guide pointed out an abandoned complex that had once produced eating utensils made of aluminum. Such a product was possible only in an economy with no alternatives. As anyone who has ever bitten on a piece of aluminum foil knows, aluminum produces an uncomfortable sensation when it comes into contact with metal tooth fillings. One must chew very carefully when using an aluminum fork.

Western German companies were also losing competitiveness. In the euphoria that followed reunification, Germans overlooked how profoundly the changes afoot challenged the West German model. The demise of the Soviet Union, along with reforms in China, radically changed the structure of the world economy. Where once German companies needed to compete primarily with European, American, or Japanese companies, now there was low-cost, increasingly skilled competition from Eastern Europe and Asia. Germans were often slow to recognize these challenges. Helmut Kohl, the chancellor who oversaw reunification and dominated German politics for nearly two decades, was no more willing than the labor-oriented Social Democrats to risk the electoral consequences of reducing unemployment benefits or making it easier for companies to hire and fire.

Germans can be innovative, but they can also be stubbornly slow to abandon their traditions. I remember being astonished when I first began living in Germany in 1994 that it was impossible to buy a cup of coffee to take away. Obviously, the problem was not that Germans lacked the technological skill to produce paper cups with plastic lids. The obstacles were psychological. Americans often think of coffee as a caffeine fix. To Germans, it was part of a ritual, marking a moment of relaxation or social interchange during the day. Coffee should be consumed from a cup at a table. If you were really in a hurry, you could drink one standing up at a bar. They found the idea of consuming coffee on the run to be mildly offensive. They did not want to sell coffee to go, even if it was what customers wanted. (Takeaway coffee has since become ubiquitous.)

China, of course, presented a challenge for all of the wealthy industrialized nations. But Germany was particularly vulnerable. The Bundesbank, the German central bank, focused relentlessly on price stability, a policy that protected the country's legions of savers. But the policy also drove up the value of the Deutschmark, as foreign investors bought marks as a hedge against inflation elsewhere. Along with high wages and social welfare costs, the strong mark created a distinct price disadvantage for German exporters. The exchange rate peaked in 1995, when a dollar was worth 1.38 deutsche marks, nearly double its value a decade earlier. Some of the country's largest companies were threatened. Volkswagen nearly went bankrupt as its cars became too expensive for middle-class buyers. Daimler, which had moved far beyond its roots in car making and into aerospace, trains, and even home appliances, began massive layoffs in the early 1990s as foreign sales faltered.

German companies took on too much debt, lulled by low, subsidized interest rates. The problem became particularly acute among mid-sized companies—the *Mittelstand*. The credit they received from a local Sparkasse savings bank or regional Landesbank came with an explicit or de facto government guarantee. It did not reflect the true risk. By the beginning of the new millennium, many German companies were overleveraged. In 1997, the amount of their own equity that German companies possessed, their *Eigenkapital*, averaged just 6 percent.[4] The other 94 percent was pledged in some way, typically to the local Landesbank. Given Germans' traditional aversion to debt, this was a shocking statistic.

The increasing commercialization of the Internet also presented challenges for German business. The ethos of the dot-com era fit awkwardly with German business traditions. Internet entrepreneurs must have an appetite for risk, be willing to fail and try again. Germany is not a country of second chances. Employers often ask to see the high school grades of job applicants. Bad grades can prevent an applicant from getting a job. To the German mind, someone who performed poorly as a child probably has character flaws that remain in adulthood. Likewise, an entrepreneur who goes bankrupt may never get another loan and may even have trouble finding a job. Aside from the barriers embedded in German society, there was, and still is, a shortage of venture capital compared to Silicon Valley. An effort by Deutsche Börse, the German stock exchange, to create a technology-oriented stock index in the late 1990s failed miserably. The so-called Neuer Markt initially boomed. But, unlike its counterpart NASDAQ in New York, the Neuer Markt's listed companies were too weak to withstand the global dot-com meltdown in 2000. Some were outright fraudulent. Comroad, ostensibly a maker of technology for auto navigation systems, grossly inflated its reported revenue by booking sales from a fictitious subsidiary in Hong Kong. An enterprising German reporter uncovered the fraud—while vacationing in Hong Kong, she went looking for the supposed subsidiary and found that it did not exist. That and other cases fatally undermined the index's credibility. In 2003, the Neuer Markt had become such a fiasco that Deutsche Börse shut it down, replacing it with the more selective and more closely controlled NEMAX 50.

Back then, the United States topped surveys of the world's most competitive countries and served as a model for the world. German managers sometimes tried to imitate American management methods and attitudes. An example was the man who became chief executive of Bertelsmann in 1998, Thomas Middelhoff. He described himself as a German with an American passport and declared his intention to convert Bertelsmann into an Internet company. Bertelsmann, by then the largest book publisher in the world, tried to launch its own answer to Amazon known as bol.com. Middelhoff's most controversial move was its acquisition of Napster, which allowed users to share music files they had uploaded to the Internet with total disregard for copy-rights—including those held by Bertelsmann's own large music unit, BMG. Bol.com failed and Middelhoff was not able to convert Napster into a platform for legitimate music sales. In 2002, Liz Mohn, wife of the aging Reinhard Mohn, the Afrika Corps veteran who had revived Bertelsmann after the war, told Middelhoff he no longer had her husband's trust. Middelhoff left. While Middelhoff's attempt to digitize Bertelsmann did not succeed, he was right that media content was moving to the Internet and that media companies needed to respond. But it would be an American, Steve Jobs of Apple, who figured out how to get people to buy music and video online.

By the beginning of the new millennium, Germany had become known as the sick man of Europe. Growth, averaging only a little more than 1 percent per year, was the slowest in Europe. The pharmaceutical industry, which had brought the world aspirin and many other important breakthroughs, no longer had a company in the top 15 worldwide. Having grown comfortable, people at all levels of society shifted their energy from building and inventing to defending their wealth and privileges. There was even a word for it: *Besitzstandswahrung*. Originally a legal term, it came to mean "clinging ferociously to what you already have." The country's future as a power in the world economy was in serious doubt.

German labor laws, which had ensured workplace peace and served as a bulwark against communism, became a burden in an age when companies needed to react quickly to changes in demand. The law that many business owners found most grating was the so-called *Kündigungschutz*, protection from being dismissed. Employees fired for incompetence or malfeasance could appeal to a special labor court, which tended to be sympathetic to workers. Use of temporary workers was severely restricted. Kündigung-schutz provided the illusion of job security, but in fact it impeded hiring. The system was particularly hard on start-up companies trying to establish themselves in the market. If a company launched a new initiative and hired new staff, it had to calculate the expense of letting them go if the new project did not work out. Managers often concluded that new ventures were not worth the risk.

In 2003, a young entrepreneur named Arndt Rautenberg, founder of a tech consulting firm in Düsseldorf, explained to me how the Kündigungschutz could kill job creation. When the dot-com bubble burst in 2000 and caused his sales to plummet, Rautenberg had to lay off several dozen people. Under German labor law, the firm was supposed to fire the people most able to find a new job—in other words, those with the most qualifications. Rather than lose his best people, Rautenberg paid the poorest performers to leave. It was a costly lesson. "My view on hiring has changed totally," Rautenberg told me. After that he outsourced as much work as he could to India. That anecdote later became part of a story that ran on the cover of *BusinessWeek*. The headline on the cover was "The Decline of Germany"—a striking reflection of how the world had come to regard the onetime powerhouse.[5]

The introduction of the euro in 1999 had created additional pressure on Germany. The rate at which deutsche marks were traded for euros, about one euro for every two marks, was too high. It made Germany a more expensive place to operate than France. But in Germany there was little political will to respond by changing the system. Some people in business warned of the need for change, but few listened. At the earnings press conferences I often attended, it was practically a ritual for the chief executive to devote part of his prepared speech to a rant about the decline of *Standort Deutschland*—business location Germany. This was the signal for the financial wire service reporters to go to the bathroom or fetch a coffee and a cheese sandwich from the buffet table in the back of the room. They knew the chief executive could be counted on not to say anything newsworthy for another ten minutes or so.

At one press conference I attended, an executive at a large engineering company complained that it took too long for Germans to graduate from university. Elementary and secondary school took 13 years, followed by a year of compulsory military service for young men. A university degree took six years, possibly followed by several more years of graduate school—with government covering tuition the whole way. By the time a German was ready to enter the workforce, he or she might be more than 30 years old. That was too long, the executive said. It was amusing to see the barrage of hostile questions hurled by the German reporters in the audience, all of whom had benefited from that same system.

Even the German engineering tradition, still largely intact, seemed sometimes to be more of a hindrance than a help. Siemens, which had become one of Germany's largest companies more than a century after its founding by Werner Siemens, correctly recognized the importance of the mobile phone industry. But Siemens, which had grown fat serving slow-moving customers like the German telephone monopoly, took too long to realize that mobile phones were destined to be a mass-market product, not a luxury good. Engineers at Siemens, based in Munich, were so bent on quality that they designed and produced their own screws. Early models took 13 hours apiece to manufacture. Siemens mobile phones were indestructible, but far too costly, and by 1998 the company had slipped to ninth place in the industry and was losing money.[6] A Finnish company, Nokia, would become the world's largest maker of mobile phones—before it, too, was displaced by a more innovative rival in the emerging market for smartphones, Apple.

German business leaders were also guilty of complacency. In the decades after the war, Germany's biggest corporations formed a mutual-protection network known unofficially as

Deutschland AG, or Germany Inc. It was, in some ways, a modern version of the old IG system, the government-sanctioned cartels that had protected the German chemical industry before World War II. Managers sat on each other's supervisory boards, and often held stakes in each other's companies. At the center of the system were Germany's largest financial institutions, including Deutsche Bank, Dresdner Bank, publicly owned Westdeutsche Landesbank, and insurers Allianz and Munich Re. Members of Deutschland AG protected each other from takeovers and generally watched each other's backs. The system had a few advantages. Banks had intimate knowledge of their customers and could make more informed lending decisions. But sometimes bank chiefs were too close to the managers they were supposed to oversee. Hilmar Kopper, the chief executive of Deutsche Bank, was also chairman of the supervisory board of Daimler. Kopper shielded Jürgen Schrempp, the Daimler chief executive, long after it was clear that the automaker's takeover of Chrysler in the United States had been a failure. Daimler, conditioned to manufacturing exquisitely engineered Mercedes-Benz luxury cars, was poorly equipped to manage a mass-market carmaker like Chrysler. By the time Schrempp was ousted and his successor, Dieter Zetsche, unwound the deal, one of Germany's signature companies had suffered long-term damage.

Deutschland AG was also closely intertwined with politics, both through personal ties and through the publicly owned banks. The boards of the Landesbanken were dominated by elected officials or people with close ties to the political establishment. Landesbanken like Westdeutsche Landesbank in Düsseldorf, also known as WestLB, or BayernLB in Munich, belonged to the largest institutions in Germany, centers of both political and financial power in their regions. They played an important role in economic development by lending money to businesses when commercial banks were unwilling to take the risk. But too often their lending decisions were influenced by local politicians anxious to preserve jobs, and they had a tendency to try to keep alive large employers that were no longer able to compete. Instead of investing in new sources of economic growth, the Landesbanken were used to keep dying businesses on life support.

A particularly grievous example involved Kirch Group, the company that Leo Kirch had built after his early success acquiring the German rights to *La Strada*, Federico Fellini's sad tale of a circus strongman. Kirch, a charming and wily son of a winemaker, went on to become the dominant source of foreign programming for Germany's public broadcasters. His legendary, climate-controlled film library was filled with television shows like *Star Trek* or films like *Lawrence of Arabia*, which he dubbed into German. When the government gave up its television monopoly in 1984, Kirch founded the first commercial broadcaster. By the turn of the millennium, he employed some 10,000 people in the Munich area, rivaling BMW and Siemens as an employer. Kirch also had close ties to leaders of the Christian Democrats and its sister party, the Christian Social Union, which dominated Bavarian politics. Kirch's friends in politics helped him enjoy an oligopoly in the German programming rights trade.

But Kirch, who had a history of betting big on borrowed money, miscalculated badly when he attempted to launch a digital pay television service in the late 1990s. Kirch had little experience dealing directly with end users, the television audience, and overestimated Germans' willingness to pay for movies and sports. Subscribers fell catastrophically short of projections, and by 2002 Kirch Group was in deep trouble. Commercial banks began withholding credit. Fearful that Kirch Group would fail, the government of Bavaria stepped in, leaning on BayernLB to loan the equivalent of about $1 billion so that Kirch could buy rights to Formula One races, in hopes of attracting more pay television subscribers.[7] Kirch eventually went bankrupt anyway, and spent the rest of his life suing Deutsche Bank for statements by the chief executive that, he claimed, undermined his credibility with other lenders.

The Kirch debacle was a severe blow to Deutschland AG. It highlighted the unhealthy relationship between banks, big business, and politics. It was a sad example of how Germany's postwar entrepreneurs had, in their dotage, succumbed to the same temptations as earlier generations. Instead of looking for new innovations, they tried to establish de facto monopolies with privileged access to capital. The failure of one of Germany's most famous companies came as others like Siemens and Daimler were trying to cope with the forces of globalization. Their crises were symbolic of the country's economic malaise, for which there did not seem to be a cure.

It had been barely a decade since the fall of the Berlin Wall had given Germans one of the rare feel-good moments in their history. Unfortunately, the euphoria had turned to complacency.

4

Renaissance

Turning around a company is hard enough. Turning around a whole nation, one as deeply troubled as Germany seemed to be at the turn of the millennium, would seem like an almost impossible task. Yet Germany succeeded. Why?

The answer is multifaceted, but essentially Germany's renaissance occurred because of a confluence of government policy, private enterprise, and labor cooperation, nurtured by a general consensus in society that change was urgent. The effort would not have succeeded without leaders willing to risk their careers, nor without an element of luck. Because Germany is a vibrant democracy, and voters tend to prefer the status quo and fear change, progress was often slow and the debate often contentious. But the final result showed, first of all, that major reform is possible in a democracy. Secondly—and this is perhaps the lesson for Americans—it showed that major change is possible when political leaders can find agreement on common national goals, even if they disagree vehemently on how to get there.

The unlikely agent of policy change was Gerhard Schröder, a lifelong Social Democrat who was elected chancellor in 1998. A canny politician unburdened by any fixed ideology, Schröder appalled his party's left wing by holding regular, informal meetings with Germany's most prominent corporate bosses, people like Jürgen Schrempp of Daimler or Jürgen F. Strube of chemical giant BASF. They typically met in swanky settings like the restaurant at Schloss Neuweier, a restored castle near the gambling and spa town of Baden-Baden.[1] They drank red wine and brandy and smoked cigars into the night. (In keeping with the Social Democrats' leftist roots, at least they were Cuban cigars.) Schröder was elected on a promise to slash unemployment, and he was smart enough to know he could not achieve that goal without making major changes in the way Germany worked, particularly the labor market. He listened to what his business pals told him.

Schröder tapped a business leader to lead a commission that would look at ways to make the job market more flexible, while preserving as much as possible of the protections Germans had come to cherish. The man was Peter Hartz, personnel director of Volkswagen. It was a clever choice. Volkswagen, one-third owned by the state of Lower Saxony where Schröder had been governor and served on the supervisory board, is known for its good relations with workers. Hartz had credibility with both labor and business. The Hartz commission formulated a series of recommendations. German workers retained much of their protection against being fired, but the new rules gave companies much more leeway to hire temporary staff who could be easily let go in a crisis. Jobless people continued to receive generous unemployment benefits for the first year of unemployment. But after that they received a much-reduced benefit, which, while generous compared to American welfare payments, left no room for luxuries and gave jobless people a much stronger incentive to look for work. The federal unemployment office was reorganized to improve counseling for people who were chronically unemployed, and make sure jobless people were trying to find work. Amid sensational press accounts of unemployed people allegedly living it up on the Spanish island of Majorca, a popular German vacation destination, people on benefits were not even supposed to take holidays.

Like the chancellor, labor leaders set aside ideology, albeit grudgingly, and took a pragmatic approach. Because of German laws ensuring workers a voice, labor leaders sat on company supervisory boards and knew what the financial reports said. Most American managers would probably recoil at the thought of allowing workers elected by their peers to sit in on board meetings, privy to discussions of corporate strategy and confidential information, and even able to control the meeting if they can find one sympathizer on the shareholder side to give them a voting majority. But now that a national effort was needed to restore economic vibrancy, the close dialogue with workers proved to be an asset. Labor unions made a bargain with employers. Under an agreement negotiated by employers led by Martin Kannegiesser, owner of a mid-sized manufacturing company, whom we will meet later in this book, unions allowed companies in difficulty more leeway to deviate from regional wage agreements. Companies could also negotiate agreements allowing workers to book overtime in the form of so-called work-time accounts. When business was slow, the workers would put in fewer hours and cash in the overtime to avoid a decline in income. In addition, workers agreed to accept very modest wage increases in return for job security. Adjusted for inflation, labor costs in manufacturing remained essentially flat for a decade. By 2011, German hourly labor costs were 31.10 euros per hour including health insurance and other benefits.[2] That was 12 percent below France. Adjusting for productivity, Germany was a cheaper place to manufacture a product in terms of labor costs than Spain, Italy, and even Greece. (Absolute wages were lower in Greece. But German workers were more productive, more than offsetting the difference.) Meanwhile, Germany offered its traditional strengths, including superior rail and road infrastructure, generally honest public officials, and a more efficient court system to settle contract disputes.

The reforms pushed through by Schröder were not popular; change could not come without political cost. The Social Democrats' left wing was enraged, and some members resigned to join a new Left Party, which merged with the party representing remnants of the communists who had ruled East Germany. Schröder left office after his party was defeated by Angela Merkel, Helmut Kohl's successor as head of the Christian Democrats, in 2005. Schröder became chairman of the company building pipelines through the North Sea that would carry Russian gas to Germany. In the German press he was portrayed as a shill for Russian strongman Vladimir Putin. That, alas, was his reward for his services to the German economy. Still, the lesson was that courageous political leaders, willing to risk their careers for the sake of the country, are essential if a country is going to change.

Peter Hartz, who oversaw the commission that authored the reforms, suffered an even worse fate. He was forced to resign amid a scandal over his role in arranging junkets abroad for Volkswagen worker representatives, sometimes accompanied by prostitutes. (In Volkswagen's case, it appears, the cooperative relationship with labor went a little too far.) Adding to the disgrace, Hartz's name has become synonymous not with the job miracle that his reforms helped create, cutting unemployment in half, but rather, with the humiliation of welfare. A person who is "on Hartz" has hit bottom. Such is politics.

These reforms, which took effect in 2005, were important, but they were not sufficient to ensure the revival of German manufacturing and exports, and remove the country from Europe's sick roster. Laws and governments can improve the conditions for business, but in a free market economy only businesses can create jobs. Even after the reforms carried out by the Schröder government, German companies still had to work with much stricter labor regulations than in the United States or Britain.

If German companies were to thrive again, they would have to do much of the work themselves. In fact, they had begun to change before the Schröder reforms took effect. The pressure on German managers was intense. Beginning in the late 1990s, buyout firms, short sellers, and other financial predators realized that Germany offered an abundance of slow-moving prey. Politicians vilified such investors as "locusts," and their machinations were not always pretty to watch. One of the most notorious was Florian Homm, a German who learned his handiwork at Harvard Business

School and several leading U.S. investment firms including Fidelity and Merrill Lynch. In the mid-1990s he launched a short-selling attack on Bremer Vulkan, Germany's largest shipbuilder, after he correctly surmised that the company was effectively bankrupt and that the local government in Bremen could no longer afford to subsidize its operations. Thousands of jobs were lost when Bremer Vulkan's main shipyard in Bremen shut down in 1997. Homm was a dubious figure who disappeared to South America for five years after his hedge fund collapsed in 2007. He was later indicted by U.S. prosecutors on charges of securities fraud and, as of this writing, is in an Italian jail awaiting extradition. But the message he and other predatory capitalists sent to other German companies was obvious and powerful: they could no longer expect government to protect them from international capitalism, for the simple reason that government no longer had the money.

The companies that survived—many did not—rediscovered the principles that had made Germany successful since the Industrial Revolution. One of these principles was innovation, often an incremental improvement in a product or the method of producing it that provided a clear competitive advantage. Another principle was concentration on the highest end of the market—the way that Krupp had built finished cannons rather than merely iron tubes, to avoid having to compete solely on price. Perhaps the most important principle was to focus on a narrow market and dominate it. Many companies, in the rush to emulate American business fads, had forgotten these principles. Some storied names had gone out of business, like consumer electronics maker Grundig, which went bankrupt in 2003 because it could not escape the middle market. Grundig televisions and audio equipment, made in Nuremburg, had no hope of competing on price with Asian manufacturers that offered equal or better quality. The lesson of Grundig was not that Germans could not make consumer electronics. Bang & Olufsen, the

Danish maker of exquisitely designed audio equipment, was proof that a European company could still make sound systems. The lesson of Grundig was that German companies were at a serious, probably fatal, disadvantage in mass markets where price was the decisive competitive factor.

Beginning in the late 1990s, large German corporations began streamlining their businesses to concentrate on what they could do well. Daimler, which had epitomized German corporate empire building, got out of the aircraft, train, and home appliance businesses, and later sold its stake in Chrysler. In the future, Daimler would only do what it does best: make premium cars and trucks. Siemens sold its mobile phone business along with a host of other businesses that were no longer profitable or profitable enough, like auto parts or information technology. Siemens focused on doing the things it did best, which included Werner Siemens' old specialty, power generation, updated to include wind power. One of the most radical examples of corporate restructuring was Hoechst, a pharmaceutical and chemicals company based in Frankfurt that had been spun off from the disgraced IG Farben conglomerate. Jürgen Dormann, Hoechst's enigmatic chief executive, merged the pharmaceutical business with Rhône-Poulenc of France in 1999 to form Aventis (later to become Sanofi-Aventis). The diverse chemical businesses were spun off or sold. Dormann had, in effect, dissolved the company in order to save it.

Simultaneously, Deutsche Bank and the other pillars of Deutschland AG began selling their shares in large German companies. Those shares had become a liability; in the future, banks would just be banks rather than centers of industrial power. Their withdrawal from direct ownership of German corporations increased the incentives for companies to focus on their most profitable businesses, rather than empire building.

There was also an element of luck in Germany's revival. China, so often perceived as a threat to the advanced economies of the West, became a prime customer for German machinery. It turned out that Chinese factories needed German equipment to produce the goods they sold in such huge quantities to American and European consumers. In addition, as more Chinese people acquired wealth, one of the first things they wanted to buy was a BMW, Audi or Mercedes. Those companies recorded astonishing increases in Chinese sales. China became the largest market for Volkswagen, Audi's parent company, and a close rival to the United States as a source of revenue for BMW and Mercedes. Moreover, China was the most dynamic example of how countries that had once been poor were now significant markets with much faster growth rates than Europe or the United States. In the German political debate, globalization was often perceived as a threat. In fact, Germany was one of the biggest beneficiaries of globalization.

Much of the change occurring in Germany during its transition from laggard to powerhouse was invisible to most people. It was taking place in mid-sized companies, with anywhere from a few dozen employees to several thousand. According to the standard definition, a *Mittelstand* company has fewer than 500 employees and less than 50 million euros in annual revenue—a category that embraces 99.6 percent of all German companies. Mittelstand companies had formed the bedrock of the German economy for centuries, and Germany has more of them as a percentage of the total economy than any other European Union country except Slovakia.[3] But it was more difficult for these smaller German companies to take advantage of the huge shifts in the world economy. The big companies could build factories and subsidiaries abroad, distancing themselves from German rules and problems. Decoupling from the domestic economy was not as easy for mid-sized companies.

These smaller firms benefited from the reforms in government policy and labor law, but often felt ignored by political leaders. They would have to take charge of their own renaissance. Not all were able to do so. The number of companies going bankrupt in Germany or seeking protection from creditors climbed steadily in the 1990s and peaked in 2003 at more than 39,000.[4] But others, the ones that survived, reduced their dependence on debt, and worked out agreements with workers that made it easier to respond to fluctuations in sales. They reemphasized innovation and learned to take advantage of a world that was much more open to commerce than it had been before 1989. Poland and other countries that had once been behind the Iron Curtain were now available as places to produce goods at lower cost, without traveling very far. The introduction in 1999 of the euro gave them a currency less prone to becoming overvalued, as had been the case with the deutsche mark. They could better compete in world markets on price. And they were able to apply information technology in a way that complemented their existing talent for export.

This transformation was taking place largely beneath the radar. For most ordinary Germans, the first years of the new millennium were painful. If creative destruction was taking place—the free market process in which efficient companies and practices displace the inefficient ones—most ordinary people could only perceive the destruction. Initially, the benefits were slow in coming. But in 2006, unemployment began to decline.[5] Consumer spending began to inch higher. Some regions of eastern Germany, like the area around Dresden, began to grow more quickly than much of western Germany. The renaissance was underway.

5

The Soul of the German Economy

One of the lessons of the decade and a half following the reunification of Germany was that it could not thrive without a vibrant *Mittelstand*, and, moreover, that mid-sized German companies were most successful when they clung to the essential values and traditions that had made the economy strong since the nineteenth century. Bertelsmann, Daimler-Chrysler, and others had shown how slavish adoption of American business dogma often led to disaster. Germany could not thrive solely on service businesses, nor was it very good at software start-ups. Germans were at their best when they were making things.

Just as Daimler refocused on making cars and truck, thousands of mid-sized German companies concentrated more diligently on what they did best. They had to. Stricter bank regulation and the demise of Deutschland AG eroded the tradition of the house bank, the local institution that served a company over decades and was based on personal relationships as much as rigorous balance sheet analysis. Smaller companies were forced to become more prudent, reducing their dependency on credit and rebuilding capital. In 2003, owners' equity—the amount of its own money that a company used to do business instead of borrowed funds— was still at a perilously low 6 percent for German Mittelstand companies. By 2010, it had tripled again to 18 percent. Among manufacturers with annual revenue of 10 million euros to 50 million euros, owners' equity was a comfortable 34 percent and still rising.[1]

Yet a simple return to the past was not an option either. Circumstances had changed radically. The world was more open, more competitive, and business had been transformed by information technology and the Internet. Germany could not avoid change, nor could it abandon its past. The secret was to adapt the best German traditions to new circumstances. How did Mittelstand companies go about doing so?

One way was to reemphasize innovation. Between 2004 and 2010, German Mittelstand companies increased spending on research and development by 70 percent, to 8.7 billion euros, according to the Cologne Institute of Economic Research. From 2008 through 2010, more than half of all Mittelstand companies launched products or processes onto the market, a greater proportion than any other country in Europe, except Switzerland.[2]

Germany's fate is closely tied to the fortunes of its Mittelstand companies. But what is a Mittelstand company, exactly? In 1996, Hermann Simon, a university professor who later formed his own consulting company, coined the term "hidden champions" to describe small, little-known German companies that offer highly specialized products and operate globally.[3] Simon's work was extremely important, not least for the way it held up a mirror to German industry and helped German managers understand in a systemic way what made them successful, knowledge that might have been largely intuitive before. The aim of this book is to unlock the secrets of German business success by focusing more intensely on a few individual companies and managers, to explore how they have been able to overcome the costs inherent to Germany and thrive as manufacturing companies. My aim is to place these entrepreneurs in the context of the revival of the German economy, since business always involves interplay with the political, legal, and social environment. I will also try to explain the origins of these companies, to show how they continually evolved in relation to changing circumstances. The point is to show not only what German companies do to be successful but how they learned to be what they are.

Ultimately, the factors that distinguish German manufacturers are impossible to reduce to a slide presentation, because so often the people themselves, their passions and idiosyncrasies, are such a key element in the narrative. But it is possible to make some generalizations. All of the people and companies described in the pages that follow share certain traits, which are closely interconnected with each other:

- They are highly international. They are not easily discouraged by the barriers they encounter when operating outside Germany. They have embraced modern technology that makes communicating across long distances and time zones vastly easier than even a few years ago.
- They have a strong emotional connection to their businesses. Getting rich is less important than building something that will last.
- They have a cooperative relationship with employees. Germany's labor-friendly laws compel them to share information about company strategy with worker representatives. So they turn this rule to their advantage by using it to foster a stronger sense of identification and commitment among employees.
- They manage for the long term. They are willing to invest in expansion or research and development even during periods when sales are slack.
- They are innovative. Research and development is central to their business strategies.
- They are premium. They aim for the high end of their markets. Being premium is a close cousin of innovation, because they must continually give their customers a reason to pay more than lower-priced competitors.
- They are highly focused. They aim for narrow markets where they can excel, and where competition is limited.
- They are perfectionists. Their goal is to offer the highest level of quality and craftsmanship in their niche, often exceeding what customers expect.
- They are cautious to a fault, with a strong aversion to debt. But—as noted above—they are capable of boldness when crisis or opportunity demands it.

In the following pages we will meet some people who exemplify these qualities and illustrate the elements of German manufacturing prowess. Each of these companies, in its own way, played a part in the renaissance of the German economy. More importantly, they are the companies that will determine whether Germany can remain a manufacturing economy in the face of continuing threats from foreign competitors and domestic complacency. To understand whether they are equal to the challenge, let us now go inside the companies themselves.

6

Boldly Cautious

In the late 1990s, Martin Kannegiesser faced a decision that, had he chosen wrong, might have put him out of business. The company founded by his father, Herbert Kannegiesser, and named for him, specialized in machines that automatically ironed and folded laundry. It was a typical niche *Mittelstand* market, seemingly obscure but essential to the industry that it served, in this case textile manufacturers. But this lucrative market was changing radically. The textile industry was moving to Asia where labor was cheap. Martin Kannegiesser had to decide whether to follow his customers there, which would mean investing in a new factory in China, or to concentrate on its other main group of customers, commercial laundries? The laundries, for their part, were demanding more sophisticated machines that could automate the whole cycle, from washing and drying through folding. Either strategy required massive investment, and Kannegiesser could not afford both.

As much as any other company its size, Kannegiesser illustrates the threats and opportunities that confronted Germany after the fall of the Berlin Wall. New markets opened, but so did new pools of low-cost labor, which ultimately lured Kannegiesser's customers out of Germany—a threat. Yet the modernization of countries that had once been poor meant there was more demand for services like commercial laundries—an opportunity. Kannegiesser's task was to overcome the threat while exploiting the opportunity.

Martin Kannegiesser is in many ways the archetype of the postwar Mittelstand manager. He inherited the company, yet he proved to be much more than just a custodian of the family legacy. He oversaw a push by the company into export markets and made acquisitions to expand the company's areas of expertise. He inherited a business and turned it into an empire.

Martin Kannegiesser is an affable, engaging man who, with his spectacles, balding head, and slightly round figure, looks like he could host a children's television show. At

71, he is a natty dresser, and was wearing a gold sport coat with a blue pattern and crisply pressed blue trousers on the day I met him in 2013. He is something of a raconteur. I never would have thought the laundry machinery industry could be interesting until I met Kannegiesser. The first time I spoke to him in 2002, he told me an anecdote about a customer of his, Fliegel Textilservice, that collected dirty laundry from the five-star Hotel Adlon and other posh Berlin hotels every day and shipped the bedsheets and towels by river barge to Poland. Polish workers, much cheaper to employ than their German counterparts, washed, dried, and ironed the laundry using Kannegiesser equipment, and then sent it by barge back to Berlin. It was a fascinating and creative example of how German entrepreneurs were taking advantage of low-cost labor in Eastern Europe.

Kannegiesser comes across as friendly and avuncular, but he is no pushover. For years, in addition to managing a rapidly expanding, globally active family business, he was the lead labor negotiator for Gesamtmetall, the association of metal industry companies that also includes Daimler, BMW, ThyssenKrupp, and other giant manufacturers. Kannegiesser was the person whom these companies trusted to represent their interests in negotiations with IG Metall, known as one of the toughest and most militant of Germany's labor unions.

In his role as a business leader, Kannegiesser played a significant role in remaking Germany's labor market and giving companies the flexibility they needed to respond to a more changeable and volatile world. In 2004, he negotiated an agreement with IG Metall known as the Pforzheim Accord, after the city in southwestern Germany where the parties met. The agreement allowed companies to deviate from industry-wide contracts in order to cope with special business circumstances, provided they offered workers something in return, such as promises to invest in local production or avoid job cuts.

When I went to company headquarters in Vlotho in July 2013, Herbert Kannegiesser, the company, was bustling. Workers were laying paving stones for an expansion of the parking lot, and the factory complex had expanded noticeably since I had been there almost ten years earlier. A few weeks before my visit, the company had dispatched a special train from a nearby rail siding to Russia carrying 42 containers full of equipment for the Olympic village laundry in Sochi, a 10 million euro order. Russia is one of 46 countries in which Kannegiesser operates. Martin Kannegiesser was also proud of having recently equipped the King Faisal Medical Center in Riyadh. Kannegiesser said he expected sales in 2013 to top 300 million euros.

A rural tableau presents itself from the window of Martin Kannegiesser's unpretentious office. On the sultry day that I visited, golden grain was ripening on a nearby hillside. The blades of a wind turbine turned slowly on a distant ridge. Even as it grew over the decades into a large multination corporation, Kannegiesser maintained its roots in Vlotho, a sleepy community in northwestern Germany. This loyalty to local roots is a characteristic of German Mittelstand companies.

By Mittelstand standards, Kannegiesser is a young company. After World War II, Martin's father, Herbert, was a refugee from a part of Germany that is now part of Poland. He landed in Vlotho more or less by accident. An engineer who had worked in the aircraft industry, Herbert Kannegiesser recognized that the textile manufacturers in the region needed machinery, so he designed cutting and ironing machines and, in 1948, founded a company to make them. Initially there were four employees, in addition to Martin Kannegiesser's mother, Irma,[1] who handled the front office. A machine that ironed newly manufactured shirts proved to be the most successful product, so Herbert Kannegiesser concentrated on that. No one else was making similar machines, and Kannegiesser grew quickly.

It was a narrow market with little competition, but also small. "Very soon," Martin Kannegiesser said of his father, "he understood that with such a small product you need a big territory."[2] Herbert Kannegiesser confronted the problem of how a small company could establish a worldwide presence. His solution was to come to an agreement with a maker of industrial sewing machines to use its worldwide sales organization. "From one day to the other my parents had a worldwide network," Martin Kannegiesser recalled. Foreign customers often came to visit in Vlotho, where the company built a factory in a former potato field. Martin Kannegiesser remembers his parents working all day, then hosting customers for dinner at their home in the evenings. Irma Kannegiesser, who spoke English well, did the cooking.

By the early 1960s, Kannegiesser had grown to a sizeable company with sales in the millions. Then the first crisis struck. This is the big risk of being a niche provider. As long as the niche exists, competition is limited and profits high. But there is always a risk that the niche will narrow into oblivion because of a sudden change in technology. And so it was with Kannegiesser. In this case, the technical innovation was one that most people regard as a convenience, but that for Kannegiesser was an existential threat: permanent-press shirts. "Orders dried up," Martin Kannegiesser said. "The little company had nothing to do."

The solution came from a customer, as it often does. "A customer came to my father and said, 'Can you press wet shirts?'" Martin Kannegiesser recalled. Even though permanent press had undercut the market for Kannegiesser ironing machines, commercial laundries needed machines to press freshly washed clothing. Herbert Kannegiesser designed a machine to do the job, and "all of a sudden he was in the laundry business," Martin Kannegiesser said. The advent of no-iron garments also affected the laundry business and services that specialized in washing and pressing shirts. So Kannegiesser moved beyond shirt pressing and developed new products, including automatic folding machines for laundries and fusing machines for the garment industry, which bond pieces of clothing together using heat and pressure.

Meanwhile, Martin Kannegiesser was studying business at the University of Cologne. It may seem surprising that the son of an engineer would choose a management and economics program, but Martin Kannegiesser had begun working for the family business as a teenager, often representing the company at trade fairs. So maybe it made sense for him to concentrate more on subjects like marketing and finance. After graduation, Kannegiesser had planned to spend five years or so getting experience at another company, then work for his parents. But his father said that would be too long. "Don't tell mother," Herbert Kannegiesser confided to his son. "But I'm not feeling well."[3]

Herbert Kannegiesser suffered a stroke when Martin was just 29, forcing the son to assume management of the business. When Herbert died four years later, in 1974, Martin became owner along with his mother. The son proved a capable and dedicated manager. He continued the international expansion begun by his father, diversifying beyond ironing into related products like tunnel finishers, which remove wrinkles from shirts without pressing. In the 1990s, Martin Kannegiesser began making acquisitions with the idea of expanding into other parts of the industrial laundry cycle. For example, in 1990 after the fall of the Berlin Wall, Kannegiesser bought a formerly state-owned maker of industrial ironing equipment.

But by the end of the 1990s, Martin Kannegiesser found himself at a crossroads. The clothing manufacturers were moving to Asia, while the large laundries were consolidating and demanding systems that could wash, dry, iron, and fold—the whole industrial laundry cycle. Kannegiesser had two options: he could follow the textile manufacturers to Asia, or he could start making the big systems that the heavy-duty laundries wanted. "The international apparel industry had changed completely," he remembered later. "Everything went offshore. Our customers had disappeared. We would have to follow them to developing countries."

It was one of those decisions that determines the fate of a company and all the people who depend on it for a living, a particularly critical question in Vlotho, which has only about 19,000 people and not a lot of other large employers. Like the advent of permanent press decades earlier, this shift in the market exposed the downside of serving a narrow, specialized market. In good times, a company like Kannegiesser can practically own the market. But there is always a risk that the niche will change shape or disappear altogether. It is a constant balancing act. The more focused a company is, the more it can concentrate its resources on doing one thing quite well. But too narrow a focus can be fatal if the market changes.

Kannegiesser was well aware of other once-famous German names that had disappeared because management had recognized trends too late. Grundig was one. It continued making televisions and radios for the mass market in Germany long after it became impossible to compete with Asian companies like Sony on price. Who but a hard-core car buff remembers Borgward? The once-storied automaker based in Bremen went bankrupt in 1961. Kannegiesser remembered. These companies recognized too late that their market had changed.

Such moments of decision require German managers to cast aside their natural caution. At the same time, Kannegiesser clung to certain principles. Bankers advised him to convert Kannegiesser into a holding company and sell stock. Consultants advised him to move operations to China. But Kannegiesser could not imagine giving up ownership. In the cyclical machinery business, it was necessary to hoard cash for slack times, and to invest heavily in innovation even when sales were poor, something that might be difficult for profit-oriented shareholders to accept. "If it's your company you don't need to justify yourself to anyone," he said.

Kannegiesser tried to diversify, producing so-called reaction injection molding machines, which are used to produce plastic parts primarily for the auto industry. But he quickly discovered that was not his business. "We didn't have the depth and the expertise," he said. Ultimately, Kannegiesser decided he did not want to spend half his time in China. Nor did he want to cut operations in Vlotho. Kannegiesser decided to stay in his hometown and concentrate on serving commercial laundries. "Sometimes you have to bet everything on one card," Kannegiesser said. He decided to concentrate on offering integrated systems that could handle the complete laundry process, and also to build up the worldwide support services that customers needed. Kannegiesser sold two of his existing divisions and instead acquired five new companies with complementary products. Kannegiesser believed that offering the complete spectrum of laundry technology, under one brand and as an integrated system, allowed him to win orders like the Olympic winter games in Russia or the King Faisal medical center.

The process that Kannegiesser went through was repeated at countless Mittelstand companies in the late 1990s and early 2000s. As a group, their competitiveness had slipped in the previous decade, and the euro, launched in 1999, initially made German products more expensive within the European Union. Companies were forced to reexamine their products and their markets and develop new strategies. Those that did so successfully were the ones that led the revival of the German economy.

Within a few years, Kannegiesser acquired other companies to fill gaps in the product line, such as heavy-duty water extractors and massive driers, or machines to fold shirts or bathrobes, or conveying systems that propel articles of laundry through pneumatic tubes from one cycle to the next. Five of the companies he acquired were in Germany, and one was in Britain. The decision to stay close to home proved to be correct. Within a short time Kannegiesser had tripled its revenue.

For a company whose goal was to be the best in the world at one thing, the lesson was that the key to surviving a big shift in the market was to focus not on products but on customers. The choice Kannegiesser faced was not really about what kind of machines to make, but which of his customer groups he could best serve. Products may become obsolete, but customers do not. Kannegiesser knew that as long as people need to wash their clothes, there would be demand for his machines. He knew how to nail his niche.

Despite his age, Kannegiesser was still intensely involved in the business when I met him in 2013. The key to future success, he said, was permanent innovation. He invests about 10 percent of sales in research and development (R&D). Lately his R&D has focused on environmental impact and energy costs. Kannegiesser was working on ways to recover more energy and water used during the laundering process, for customers under increasing economic, regulatory, and social pressure to be more sustainable. Software was another big area of research, Martin Kannegiesser said. Kannegiesser machines can, for example, detect whether a hotel bed sheet has a hole in it. The company also supplies systems that help laundries track articles as they pass through the system, and there are systems that can sort clothing by color—for example, separating green surgical clothing in a hospital from white nurses' uniforms. The company can diagnose problems with its machines remotely, and supervise repairs from afar. Kannegiesser fretted about how to attract the best code writers to Vlotho, with its lack of urban amenities, to write the software for such products. "We are trying to get as many software people as we can," he said. "It's not easy."

Kannegiesser machines are a marvel to watch, especially for anyone who hates doing laundry and wishes it could all be done by robots. Kannegiesser washing machines can hold up to four tons of dirty laundry. Its automatic ironing machines can press 1,200 hotel bed sheets or complimentary bathrobes in an hour. The company makes systems that can wash, spin, dry, and press laundry by the barge-full—literally, as his Berlin customer proved. The machines themselves are complex, requiring considerable engineering skill to manufacture.

Because of his years as a top negotiator and a prominent public figure, Kannegiesser was able to think about overreaching trends that would affect not only his business but the country as a whole. He was concerned about demographics, about Germany's aging and shrinking population, which made him especially keen to hold onto his people and also train new ones. He was proud that some of his apprentices were third-generation Kannegiesser workers. The country was going to have to get used to more immigration, he said, and employers were going to have to make it easier for employees to balance their lives and their work, to hold onto working parents. He could not afford to lose skilled people.

He was grateful for the German short-work program that helped companies avoid layoffs during the 2009 recession that followed the financial crisis in the United States and Europe. The government program allowed companies to cut worker hours and made up some of the lost wages with public aid. "If you break up a team, it is so hard to rebuild that," Kannegiesser said.

Kannegiesser has only a few major competitors, such as Jensen Group, based in Belgium. But new competition is always a threat. Asian companies make less sophisticated machines and are trying to move up the technological ladder. Some U.S. companies compete in some market segments. In his industry, Martin Kannegiesser said, the key is not to be focused on a particular product but on the needs of customers in a narrowly defined market. "We consider ourselves as system integrators," he said. "Being focused today means you can solve a complete problem set for a customer, not just one single product."

7

"We're Never the Cheapest"

If you are a museum curator and your job is to make sure that King Tut's mummy lasts several more millennia, you probably do not cut corners on his final resting place. You buy the best, which in the opinion of quite a few museums comes from a company located across from a Fiat dealership in a cluttered commercial neighborhood of Frankfurt. Deep in his tomb in Luxor, Egypt, the Boy King rests in a vitrine made by Glasbau Hahn, founded in 1836 and still run by the same family. Cases made by Glasbau Hahn also hold copies of the Declaration of Independence at the New York Public Library or Etruscan artifacts at the British Museum, to name just a few examples.

Price is secondary to a museum curator entrusted with a Gutenberg Bible, says Till Hahn, the family patriarch. "In 20 years, no one will ask what the vitrine cost," Hahn says. "What matters is the preservation of the object."[1]

Germany has not been a cheap place to do business since the nineteenth century, and the most successful German companies learned long ago to set themselves apart by being more innovative than their customers and aiming at markets where price was secondary. Glasbau Hahn has a long tradition of innovation. According to family tradition, Till Hahn's grandfather won a prize at the Paris Expo in the 1800s for a special kind of leaded glass. During the 1930s, Glasbau Hahn perfected a method for joining two pieces of glass without a frame. In 1965, the company devised a new way to build windows, suspending the glass from the top of the frame, which made it possible to design buildings with much larger glass surfaces. More recently, Glasbau Hahn has developed ways to make display cases that are dustproof and airtight enough to keep King Tut surrounded by nitrogen gas, which minimizes the risk of decay and improves his chances of lasting another few thousand years.

One thing that almost all German companies have in common, from a giant like Daimler to a workshop operation like Glasbau Hahn, is that they are not the low-price or even mid-price competitors in their market segments. With a combination of technology, innovation, precision, and a touch of marketing cachet, they succeed because they are able to convince customers that their products are worth more. "We're never the cheapest," says Hahn, a cheerful 72-year-old who favors corduroys and argyle sweaters.

Visiting Glasbau Hahn, it is hard for one to believe it is a market leader with a global reputation. The company headquarters could easily be mistaken for one of the auto repair shops or plumbing supply outlets that characterize its rapidly gentrifying neighborhood a few miles from Frankfurt's banking quarter. There are 140 employees. When I visited one time, one of Till Hahn's grandchildren was running loose around the front office.

The homey atmosphere is misleading. Glasbau Hahn is another example of a German mini multinational, generating over two-thirds of its sales abroad and dominating its narrow niche. Companies like Glasbau Hahn are the reason that Germany's trade surplus is by far the largest in Europe. Despite their small size, companies like Glasbau Hahn learned long ago to compensate for slow domestic growth by expanding overseas. Glasbau Hahn exhibited at the St. Louis World's Fair in 1905, Till Hahn says, though it would be another half a century before the United States became an important market. To offset the relatively high cost of labor in Germany, companies have no choice but to concentrate on premium products for which customers are willing to pay extra.

Of course, practically any company would like to be the premium brand in its market. What is the secret of actually becoming one?

Clear focus on a market segment is one obvious precondition. The trick is to find and identify those segments. Ideally, your product should dominate the high end of the market not only in your region but globally as well. Once that exclusive real estate has been conquered, defending it requires constant vigilance. When the market changes, as it almost always will, a company has to be ready to move into new or narrower segments.

Glasbau Hahn began as a simple glazing workshop in 1836. Its path into the market for museum display cases began before World War II, when Till Hahn's father, Otto, began applying the company's expertise to make display cases for department stores. When retailers proved reluctant to pay for the level of quality that Glasbau Hahn offered, Hahn père hit on the idea of selling the vitrines to museums. The first sale was in 1937.

When Till Hahn came of age in the 1950s, he was given responsibility for the display case business. Americans were a major presence in Frankfurt then. The city, still badly damaged by bombing, was the headquarters for the U.S. military. The U.S. Army took over a campus-like office complex in the city's West End that had been previously occupied by the IG Farben conglomerate, infamous for manufacturing the Zyklon B gas used in the Nazi gas chambers. (More recently, the complex has been converted into a campus for Goethe University's finance school.)

A watercolor on one wall of Till Hahn's office depicts what little was left of Glasbau Hahn's workshops at the end of World War II. But despite the damage the company had suffered at the hands of the allies, Otto Hahn seems to have accommodated himself quickly to the new occupiers. From a cabinet, Till Hahn retrieves samples of souvenir glass coasters that the company sold to U.S. GIs after the war, as it scrambled to cope with the economic collapse that followed German capitulation. According to Till Hahn, Otto Hahn had never been drafted into the Wehrmacht and was regarded as untainted by Nazi crimes.[2] He spoke English, and was even able to strike up an acquaintance with General Lucius D. Clay, the military governor in the American zone. Still, when Till Hahn suggested that America might be a fertile market for Glasbau Hahn display cases, his father thought that was a dumb idea. "The Americans don't appreciate quality," Till Hahn recalls his father saying. "It has to be fast and cheap."[3]

Till Hahn was able to prove his father wrong during a trip to the United States in the late 1950s, the *Bildungsreise* then and now considered an essential part of the education of an ambitious young German business person. Till Hahn travelled from Boston to Key West, visiting, he says, 200 museums. "The stereotype that Americans have no sense of quality, in our market that was not true," Hahn says. On the contrary, many museums kept their best pieces locked up in their basements, for lack of a safe way to display them. "I was always welcomed with open arms. I said, 'This is a place where we have a chance.'" It was, in retrospect, an audacious bit of marketing by a young man barely 19, and illustrates how German business people have never felt constrained by the borders of their own country or been afraid to venture into strange lands. America quickly became one of Glasbau Hahn's biggest markets. The company recently supplied display cases for a renovation of the New York Metropolitan Museum of Art's Islamic Galleries.

For Glasbau Hahn and other German exporters, there is always the risk that, having demonstrated that there is a market for their specialized products, they will spawn local competitors. It was with some trepidation that Glasbau Hahn entered China in 2005, displaying its products at trade shows and investing a modest sum to open a representative office. Indeed, within a few years a Chinese company was producing exact copies of Glasbau Hahn vitrines. Yet the competition had little effect. Most display cases are tailor-made for the specific needs of the customer, and the competitor lacked the expertise to provide the same custom service. Glasbau Hahn typically dispatches teams from Frankfurt to install its display cases, though they often work with local helpers. "Our specialty is that we build to order, and you can't copy that," says

Isabel Hahn, Till's daughter, who now runs the company with her cousin, Tobias Hahn.

Nor could any local competitor advertise that its products were "Made in Germany." Even in China, the German brand commanded respect. Isabel Hahn recalls one Chinese customer who insisted that even the screws used in its display cases should be made in Germany. She had to tell the customer that, alas, even German companies manufacture their screws in China these days.

Retaining possession of the high end of the market requires constant struggle. Though museum display cases are Glasbau Hahn's most famous product and generate the most sales, the company also produces custom-made windows at a separate factory in Stockstadt am Main, about 40 kilometers, or 25 miles, southeast of Frankfurt. In the 1970s, the Arab oil crisis prompted the German government to tighten energy standards for business and require that windows be double-paned for better insulation. The new regulations undercut the value of Glasbau Hahn's technology for making very large windows, which had proven especially popular with builders of airports. The construction method, in which the glass was suspended from the top of the frame, was ill-suited to double-pane glass. Till Hahn responded by designing louvered windows with smaller frames inside a larger one, to fill large surfaces with double-paned glass. Hahn thought the windows were ugly, but when he showed them at trade fairs, architects loved the geometric patterns of the frames within a frame. The product was a hit, and remains an important line of business. Glasbau Hahn also has a department that provides custom glass engineering for specialized construction projects, such as glass staircases or elevator shafts shrouded in glass. Glasbau Hahn diligently avoids any market where it is not possible to be the premium supplier. At one point Glasbau Hahn sold armoured glass. But when larger companies began mass-producing similar products, Glasbau Hahn got out. "We had no advantage," Till Hahn says.

Glasbau Hahn illustrates another characteristic of German business. It has applied an engineers' mentality to a seemingly mundane object. Its vitrines have elaborate dust-protection and climate control systems. The glass panels slide open with the touch of a remote control. One new product line, called Hahn Pure, uses materials that minimize any danger to display objects from chemicals in the glass which might leach into the atmosphere itself. Such features help keep the product exclusive.

It often seems that there is nothing that escapes the German mania for engineering. Falke, another family company, has done it for socks. Rösle has done it for garlic presses, spatulas, and other kitchen implements, while pencil and pen maker Faber-Castell has created a pen made of gold leaf and ancient wetland oak that sells for $4,700. Such prices are justified in part by their exquisite design and engineering.

Surprisingly, however, Isabel Hahn, a warm, thoughtful woman with brown hair who balances her managerial duties with motherhood, said she has become convinced that engineering is not what really sets German companies apart. "I used to think that our specialty was know-how," Isabel Hahn says. "I have changed my mind completely. Now I think it's craftsmanship."

The emphasis on craftsmanship, on attention to detail, and a striving for perfection help explain why many German companies are extraordinarily reluctant to let go of workers—the actual craftsmen and craftswomen. There is an element of loyalty, but also self-interest. When a company is focused on a narrow niche, the skills it requires are equally specialized. A master glazer at Glasbau Hahn represents years, even decades of training and experience that is difficult to replace.

The accord that German labor unions struck with employers early in 2004, Martin Kannegiesser's Pforzheim Accord, established the framework for companies and workers to work out special agreements at the local level.

The accord made it easier for managers to react to fluctuations in demand, providing more job security to workers. Flexibility is especially important to German companies because so many of them make capital goods, products that are designed to be used for many years and require a large up-front investment. Such markets tend to be very sensitive to economic cycles, because customers may postpone large purchases during periods of recession or slow economic growth. Glasbau Hahn's business is highly sensitive to the fortunes of the donors who finance acquisitions and new wings for many of the world's museums.

Although Glasbau Hahn workers are not unionized, the company as well as its workers are among those who benefited from the increased flexibility available after 2004. The company managed to avoid any layoffs during the severe slump in 2009 that followed the collapse during the previous year of investment bank Lehman Brothers. Glasbau Hahn deployed so-called work-time accounts, a widely used tool that was one of the innovations of the Pforzheim agreement. Employees bank overtime hours during busy periods. When business is slow, they work less but draw on the accounts to keep receiving the same pay.

"Last year we had too little work, this year we have too much," said Till Hahn, when I first met him in 2010. A few years later, Isabel Hahn admitted that she suffered sleepless nights worrying about the business and her responsibility to her employees and the family legacy. This is the downside of being highly specialized. There is little room for error. Bankruptcies among Mittelstand manufacturers are not uncommon, though they are less likely to go bust than German retailers or builders. For every 10,000 manufacturers, 66 filed for insolvency in the first half of 2013, less than two-thirds the rate of the other industries.[4] Pickhan, the fabricator of Richard Serra sculptures mentioned earlier in this book, suffered a crisis in 2009, which was a brutal year for many German companies. Orders from the United States and Europe dried up after the collapse of Lehman Brothers, and the financial crisis that followed. In Pickhan's case, the company survived by finding a new owner, but many other companies were not so lucky. Mittelstand managers know they must be constantly alert to new threats.

The internationalization of German companies is one of the country's great strengths, but it also can make firms vulnerable to political and economic turmoil. King Tut's modern homeland was an example. When I met the Hahns again in mid-2013, Egypt was convulsed by political turmoil after the military deposed the Islamist government. "I'm feeling much more vulnerable to politics," Isabel Hahn said. She was looking for a new line of business to augment the vitrine business. "We need a new market, so we're not so dependent on museums," she said. She didn't yet know what the new line of business would be, but it would have to draw on Glasbau's Hahn's expertise in working with glass, the one constant ever since the company began operating under the Hahn name in 1870. Said Till Hahn, "It has to be connected to our core competence." Said Isabel Hahn, "It has to be something unique. It has to have a unique selling point." And it would not be the cheapest.

8

Mini Multinationals

A wooden pallet sits on the shop floor of Bollin Armaturenfabrik, stacked with cardboard boxes marked "China." Nearby, workers stand at lathes, polishing and grinding fixtures that look like something to which you would attach a garden hose. As odd as it may seem, Bollin in fact exports handmade faucets to China and other developing countries from its workshop on the outskirts of Frankfurt. They are, of course, not just any faucets. They are made of special alloys and machined to exquisitely fine tolerances, for use in places like oil refineries or chemical factories where failure of the product could shut down the plant—or worse. "That's going to Beijing on Friday," a shop foreman said, gesturing toward a pallet and speaking above the whir of metal lathes and drill presses.[1]

Although it has only about 30 employees, Christian Bollin Armaturenwerk is a multinational company. Dagmar Bollin-Flade, granddaughter of the founder, and her husband and business partner, Bernd Flade, serve customers all over the world from a modest workshop set back from the street in a working-class neighborhood of Frankfurt. There is a pharmacy across the street and an Asian grocery store a few doors down. Dagmar spent part of her childhood living in an adjacent apartment house, and played in a small courtyard next to the workshop. The setting is humble, but Bollin Armaturenfabrik is proof that even very small companies can exploit the global marketplace. The company also shows that operating internationally does not have to entail huge risk. On the contrary, Dagmar Bollin-Flade and Bernd Flade are exceedingly cautious people who run their business with extreme prudence.

German companies have been export oriented since at least the nineteenth century, but in the last decade, new technology has supercharged their ability to operate globally. The Internet makes it cheap and easy to communicate with customers across time zones and to exchange technical specifications generated by computer-aided design

(CAD) software. Express shipping services like DHL, which belongs to Deutsche Post, the German postal service, make it possible to deliver products in small batches quickly and cheaply anywhere in the world. Fast shipping is crucial for Bollin Armaturenfabrik, which produces high-end industrial faucets to order for customers that often need the parts within days if not hours. The market for such products is narrow—a typical *Mittelstand* niche business. But it is a lucrative market for a company that can tap the global market. Its being located in Germany, with its relatively high labor costs, is no disadvantage. Customers will pay what they have to for a component that may be essential to keep a factory running. "The price is not the issue. Delivery time is the issue," Bollin-Flade says. "There aren't too many companies that do what I do."[2]

The euro, introduced in 1999, reinforced German companies' long tradition of operating abroad. The common currency meant that they no longer had to worry about exchange-rate fluctuations when doing business with other euro zone countries. About 30 percent of Bollin's sales are outside Germany but inside the Eurozone. Within the Eurozone, Germany is often a cheaper place to produce because other countries have allowed wages to rise faster than productivity.

The euro has also removed some of the price disadvantage of operating in Germany. The common currency has tended to be weaker against the dollar than the deutsche mark used to be, which makes it easier for German companies to compete when doing business outside the Eurozone. "That gave us a huge impetus," Bollin-Flade says. The travails of Greece, Italy, and other countries in recent years have given the euro something of a bad name, but Bollin-Flade is keenly aware of the economic benefits of a common currency. She and most of her Mittelstand peers feel no nostalgia for the days when they and their customers had to keep an eye on the value of a dozen European currencies, when the German deutsche mark sometimes became so strong that it threatened to price them out of foreign markets. "All those who say 'We want to get out of the euro'—they don't remember how it was," Bollin-Flade says.

Bollin-Flade's stature in Germany is greater than the size of her company would suggest. For many years she was the chairman of the Mittelstand Committee of the Association of German Chambers of Commerce and Industry, one of the country's most powerful business groups. She has been invited to discuss Mittelstand issues with Angela Merkel, the German chancellor. When I spoke to Bollin-Flade in June 2013, she had recently been to Berlin to meet with Peer Steinbrück, who was the lead candidate of the main opposition party, the Social Democrats, in national elections that fall. (Merkel's party, the Christian Democrats, won the vote and she remained chancellor in a coalition with the Social Democrats.) Bollin-Flade doubts that she has had much influence on government policy—politicians like to be photographed with Mittelstand managers, but do not necessarily pay much attention to their concerns. At least, Merkel, a pastor's daughter who grew up in communist East Germany, seems to have absorbed Mittelstand values, or maybe she had them all along. She often seems to run Germany as if it were a provincial machine-tool supplier. She aims for stability more than growth. Debt is bad; prudence a higher virtue than profit.

Even by German standards, Bollin Armaturenfabrik is exceedingly cautious. A few years ago, Bollin-Flade did something that probably would have gotten her drummed out of the local chamber of commerce in Silicon Valley or Shanghai. She turned down orders from her biggest customer. Bollin-Flade was worried about becoming too dependent on any one source of revenue. So she and her husband and business partner, Bernd Flade, enforced a rule they still apply today: no customer may account for more than 10 percent of sales, even if that sometimes means turning away business. "If 20 percent of your sales fall away, that's difficult," Bollin-Flade says. "If 10 percent falls away it's not nice, but it's not dramatic." They felt vindicated when the big customer later went bankrupt. Needless to say, they also avoid getting in debt. "My machines are paid for," Bollin-Flade says. "I have no bank credit. That's what sets the Mittelstand apart. You set aside something for bad times."

The German approach has often annoyed its Eurozone partners, who wished German taxpayers were more willing to share their wealth. At least, German consumers could spend a little more, could they not? But arguably the German approach protected the country during the Eurozone crisis and helped it avoid downturns like those that hit Spain and Italy. While Greece was racking up debt during the 2000s, Mittelstand companies were resolutely cutting theirs. "We're not feeling the crisis," Bollin-Flade told me.

While Germany's economic might is often cause for jealousy and resentment, it is questionable whether the euro monetary union could have survived the crisis in recent years without it. Companies like Bollin Armaturenfabrik are arguably more important than giants like Siemens and Daimler in determining whether the German economy can continue to act as locomotive for the Eurozone. German Mittelstand companies are far from invulnerable. Bankruptcies were rising steeply in 2013. The number of insolvencies among companies with annual sales of 5 million to 25 million euros rose more than 22 percent in the first half of 2013. In absolute numbers, 820 companies went bust compared to 670 in the same period a year earlier.[3]

Yet there are also reasons to believe that the Mittelstand is well armored for the future. The turmoil of the twentieth century, the years of stagnation that followed German reunification, and then the sharp recession in 2009 taught Mittelstand companies always to be prepared for the worst.

Caution by Mittelstand owners should not be mistaken for timidity. Bollin-Flade, who has two grown sons, was one of three women in a class of about 400 engineering students at the Technical University of Darmstadt. She had graduated from an all-girls high school and the male-female ratio in the engineering school was a bit of a shock. Bollin-Flade probably would have found more female company in a business management program, but did not think she would get the skills she needed to take over from her father. She had no brothers, and it was important to keep the business in the family. "I thought, if I'm going to take over this company, I don't want anyone to have to explain the technology to me," Bollin-Flade says. "I wouldn't have been able to make decisions. I didn't want to be dependent on anyone." The company still gets calls asking for "Herr Bollin."

She and Bernd met at engineering school. They share a modest office decorated with portraits of Bollin-Flade's father and grandfather. As we talked, Bernd worked at a computer, often interjecting an opinion or observation. They agreed that they prefer to keep the company small and uncomplicated, which makes it easier to respond quickly to customer needs. "If a customer calls with a request," Bernd said, "I speak to the workshop manager, and it's done." The company aims to respond to a customer request with a price quote within half an hour and, according to Bernd, succeeds 86 percent of the time.

The company began expanding abroad in the 1960s, following large customers such as Linde, a maker of industrial gases. Initially Bollin Armaturenfabrik supplied German companies, but then began to find foreign customers. Bollin-Flade was a child then and remembers visits from Indians and people from the Middle East, and even customers from the Soviet Union. She said she learned not to be judgmental or condescending in dealing with foreigners. Today Bollin Armaturenwerk has freelance sales representatives in 22 countries. When there is a need to visit one of the reps or a customer abroad, Bernd is usually the one who goes.

The firm bought its first computer in the mid-1980s. Bollin-Flade admits that Mittelstand companies were a bit slow to embrace information technology, but those days are over. Bollin-Flade now has a database of over 200,000 technical drawings, based on pieces it has produced in the past. Usually, when a customer has a request, an existing design can be reused or modified to do the job. The CAD software also helps automate much of the actual production work. Using the technical specifications, a computer tells the lathe or another machine what to do. Still, a human has to supervise the process, and there remains an element of craftsmanship. The same worker who sets up a machine is also responsible for producing the component. "That leads to a very high sense of identification," Bernd Flade says. "Every lathe operator says, 'That is my piece.'"

To the unprofessional eye, Bollin's products look like the kind of faucet to which you would attach a garden hose. But they may cost thousands of euros each, and are made to regulate the flow of gases and liquids in power plants, chemical refineries, or other places where pressures and temperatures may be extreme. A defective component can shut down production or even cause an explosion.

Bollin Armaturenwerk has also confronted shifts in the market, where it was forced to make a decision with existential implications for the company. In the early 1990s, for example, competitors began producing faucets out of machined, rectangular blocks of metal known as bar stock. Until then, pieces had been made out of forged blanks, which were more expensive and therefore more profitable for Bollin. For their narrowly defined industry, the advent of bar stock was a huge and potentially threatening innovation. Dagmar and Bernd said they spent six months mulling whether to start offering pieces made from bar stock. It was a continuous dinner table topic. Eventually they decided that, if customers wanted bar-stock pieces, they should supply them. Forged pieces still account for a majority of orders, however.

The company website has become an important marketing tool, and an example of how technology has helped
German companies become even more export-oriented
than they already were. Bollin even engages in search-
engine optimization, to raise the chances of showing up
high on the list when a panicked power-plant operator in
Indonesia Googles "custom manifold fast delivery."

Bollin has profited from German economic reforms,
which made it easier to use temporary workers. But
Dagmar Bollin-Flade worries that much of the political
debate is about restoring treasured social services and not
about making Germany even more competitive. "People are
always talking about rolling back the reforms," she says. "We
have to go in the other direction."

In part, the frugality and caution of companies like
Bollin Armaturenfabrik reflect the insecurity they live with.
Both Dagmar and Bernd often work long hours. Time zone
differences sometimes require them to be on the job at 4
a.m. or late in the night. They do not live extravagantly.
"You can only wear one pair of pants," says Dagmar, who
favors pantsuits. "The second one is in the closet, and you
don't need the third." While one must always be careful with
national stereotypes, it is true that Germans are among the
world's biggest savers. In their minds, it seems, the next crisis is always around the corner. Bollin Armaturenfabrik has
enough cash to last the better part of a year without revenue,
Dagmar Bollin-Flade says, a practice that came in handy in
the sudden slump in orders that came at the end of 2008. "If
you lean back and say, 'I've earned my money,' in one year,
three years, you're out of business," she says.

Little Swabia and the Art of Global Manufacturing

There are so many companies from southwestern Germany with factories in Taicang, China, near Shanghai, that the area is known as Little Swabia. Most are machinery makers like Trumpf, a company based in Ditzingen, Germany, that produces equipment used to cut and form metal with lasers. Trumpf built a plant in Taicang in 2009, and has expanded it several times since because sales have grown so fast. When Trumpf's European sales plunged in 2008 because of the financial crisis, China quickly took up the slack and then some. Executives at the company, managed by the wife and husband team of Nicola Leibinger-Kammüller and Mathias Kammüller expect China eventually to become their largest market.

This is the flip side of the rise of China to become the world's largest exporter. The products that China sells to the United States and elsewhere are often made in factories equipped wall-to-wall with German machines. That is one reason why Germany's trade deficit with China is proportionally much smaller than most other developed countries. If sales by German companies producing in China were included, Germany would be one of the only countries in the world to have a trade surplus with China.

As we have seen, exports have long been crucial to German industrial companies because of the limited size of their domestic market. As their exports grow, German companies often must confront the question of whether they should produce abroad, and if so, how much. The question became more urgent after the fall of the Berlin Wall opened up Eastern Europe for production and sales, and more urgent still after China, India, and other developing countries became important markets as well as efficient places to produce.

The answer is different for different companies. Some, like Herbert Kannegiesser, have elected to keep production close to home, where they can more easily oversee quality and protect their innovations. Kannegiesser has sales and service offices in China, however, and Martin Kannegiesser said he does not rule out producing in China sometime in the future. Right now, "to transfer all the know-how would require so much effort" that it would not make business sense, Kannegiesser said.

Other companies, like the carmakers Daimler, BMW and Volkswagen, have built factories all over the world, including in China, while maintaining a critical mass of production in Germany. The strong connection to Germany helps preserve their Made in Germany identity, as well as access to engineers coming out of German universities, and to German *Mittelstand* supplier networks, which are an important part of the innovation process. At the same time, by shifting some production abroad, companies move closer to their foreign customers. They learn more about the market and shorten delivery times and costs. They also protect themselves from currency fluctuations, in what is known as natural hedging. Companies often save on labor costs, too, although low wages alone are rarely sufficient reason to move abroad.

Trumpf offers a good view of the risks, benefits, and challenges of producing abroad. With annual sales of 2.35 billion euros in 2013, Trumpf is a substantial corporation. But it remains in family ownership, and is managed along Mittelstand principles. Trumpf has had a significant presence in the United States since the late 1960s with a manufacturing facility in Farmington, Connecticut, and is well acquainted with the challenges of manufacturing far from the home base. The company also provides something of a microcosm of German postwar economic history, and indeed the evolution of the machinery industry worldwide, so it is worth traveling back in time a few decades to examine the company's origins and growth.

Like so many formidable German companies, Trumpf began in a workshop, in this case in Stuttgart, and grew fairly slowly until the day it came under the influence of an energetic and visionary young leader, a young man named

Berthold Leibinger. Trumpf had been in existence for about a quarter century when Leibinger joined as an apprentice in 1950. Then run by one of its founders, Christian Trumpf, the company specialized in motorized hand-held shears and other tools for cutting and shaping sheet metal. When Leibinger joined, Trumpf had 145 employees and 1 million deutsche marks in annual sales, the equivalent of about $240,000 at the time.[1]

World War II was still a very recent memory. Berthold Leibinger had been 14 when the war ended, too young for military service even by Nazi standards. But, he recalled later, he was old enough to absorb Nazi propaganda and its view that Germany was destined to rule the world. After Germany was defeated and the Nazi lie was exposed, young people of Leibinger's generation—at least the more enlightened ones—were overwhelmed with feelings of shame. "We were driven by the need to show that there was another Germany, a Germany of understanding and openness," Leibinger recalled years later, at age 82. "The generation immediately connected with the defeat of the war, which had experienced hunger and poverty, that shaped them."[2] Leibinger channeled those sentiments into business, and told me they were a key source of his ambition and entrepreneurial drive.

In those days, American was the undisputed superpower, not only militarily but also economically. Leibinger was determined to see for himself how Americans did things. In 1957, after his studies in mechanical engineering at the Technical University of Stuttgart, which he completed while continuing to work at Trumpf, Leibinger and his new wife, Doris, headed to America. Leibinger presented himself at the Cincinnati Milling Machine Co., which then employed 6,000 people and was the largest machine tool company in the world. As he steered his Volkswagen Beetle to the headquarters building in Cincinnati, with its façade of stylized columns and an American flag fluttering prominently from a tall mast out front, "I was overwhelmed by the grandeur," Leibinger later remembered.

Of course, decades later it would be Trumpf and German companies like it that would come to dominate the machine tool industry. Leibinger, who got a job at a Cincinnati Milling factory in Wilmington, Ohio, noticed even then that his German training was superior to what his American colleagues had received. Today, Cincinnati Milling is known as Milacron, and it specializes in machines for processing plastics. With sales of about $800 million in 2011, it was about one-quarter the size of Trumpf. The two companies could be said to symbolize the declining importance of U.S. companies in the manufacture of machinery, and the ascendancy of Germany. In 2011, German production of machine tools was three times that of the United States.[3] And that figure probably understates the degree to which the Germans dominate the high end of the market.

Berthold Leibinger returned to Trumpf in 1961 and took over the six-person design department, the beginning of a career that would make him something of a legend in German industry, someone whose business acumen was in demand outside his own company. Leibinger later served on the supervisory boards of BMW and Deutsche Bank, and was president of the German Engineering Association, known by its German initials, VDMA.

By 1978, when he was 48, Leibinger was not only the chief executive of Trumpf but had also gradually acquired majority ownership from Christian Trumpf. Leibinger could boast of numerous patents and product innovations. The most famous and significant, by far, was his exploitation of another American invention, the laser. Anyone interested in the saga of Trumpf's development of laser cutting machines should read Leibinger's memoirs, *Who Could Wish for Any Other Time But This*. For our purposes, suffice it to say that it was a bold move for a company that, in the late 1970s, had a secure and profitable position in its niche, the production of machines that used so-called nibbling technology to cut metal. After initially buying lasers from a U.S. supplier, and finding them inadequate to the needs of Trumpf customers, the company made the decision to produce its own. It did so with technical help from the nearby German Aerospace Center, in Stuttgart-Vaihingen, and financial support from the Federal Ministry of Science and Technology. After introducing the first commercial machines with lasers in 1979, Trumpf continually developed laser-based products until, by 2008, they accounted for 70 percent of sales, some 1.5 billion euros a year.

The new laser products "catapulted the firm into yet another new dimension," Leibinger later recalled. Why was Trumpf capable of this technological warp shift, from nibbling to beams of high intensity light, when others were not? In his memoirs, Berthold Leibinger tried to explain the process that led him to develop innovations that made some of his own proudest machine designs obsolete. "Curiosity comes top of the list," he wrote. "One has to want to know the unknown. One needs imagination to know what the new can do. Also, the courage to take a risk. And the readiness to question the tried and tested and to leave it behind. And one has to be lucky as well."[4]

In 2005, Leibinger turned over day-to-day management of the company to one of his daughters, Nicola Leibinger-Kammüller. Berthold's son Peter became deputy chief executive. Mathias Kammüller, Nicola's husband and Berthold's son-in-law, became executive vice president and head of the machine tool division. Critics might call the succession a case of modern-day dynastic succession, but the presence of three family members on the six-person management board helped ensure that Trumpf would not be listed on the stock exchange or sold to a private equity company, but would remain in the hands of people who could afford to manage with an eye to the long-term future and invest in the company at the expense of dividends—if they so chose.

Which brings us back to China. Trumpf had had representatives in China since the 1990s, and in 2002 set up a so-called job shop in Taicang. The job shop produced cut pieces of sheet metal on Trumpf machines primarily for German companies. Trumpf became a components supplier, rather than just a maker of machines, because no local companies could, at that time, offer the precision and quality that German firms operating in China wanted. When Chinese companies wanted to buy their own Trumpf machines, the orders were filled with machines made in Germany or America. But Trumpf's sales representative in China complained that delivery times were too slow. There was also a need for machines that were simpler and cheaper and more accessible to Chinese customers. And Chinese customers, just like their counterparts in Europe and America, wanted to be able to visit the factory where the machines were made, to assure themselves of the quality. "Customers wanted to see the production," Mathias Kammüller says. "It helps build confidence."[5]

Certainly the Chinese market was impossible for anyone in the machine-tool business to ignore. The Chinese factories that produced such massive quantities of consumer goods for the United States and Europe needed machines for the assembly lines, and China did not have the expertise—yet—to build those machines itself. By 2010, China was the largest buyer of machine tools in the world by a wide margin.

I expected Mathias Kammüller to tell me tales of the misadventures Trumpf encountered building a factory in a developing country like China, but that was not the case. "There are always problems, but there were no really big difficulties," Kammüller said. The local provincial government was already following a strategy of trying to attract German companies, having recognized that the Germans would be reliable employers who, once they made the investment, would stick around. Local officials were experienced in dealing with German needs, and they proved to be fast and flexible. Trumpf was lucky to find an excellent local manager, Kammüller says, and there was such an oversupply of trained engineers that Trumpf could afford to hire them as ordinary machine operators. There was no culture clash between Trumpf's German managers and the Chinese, according to Kammüller; their mentality, at least when it came to machine tools, was similar. The presence of so many other German companies in Taicang meant that Trumpf had a better supplier network than it enjoys in the United States.

The factory in Taicang began operations in 2009. Demand was so strong that Trumpf quickly ran out of capacity, and has continually expanded the plant since. Trumpf has also begun developing machines in China for the Chinese market, based on components from Germany but simplified so that they are substantially cheaper. In fact, China is the only place where Trumpf can produce more inexpensively than in Germany, because of labor costs about one-quarter the German level, in addition to an abundant supply of qualified people. Trumpf is able to manage its Taicang operation, with about 600 employees, with a relatively small crew of about 20 expatriate managers and technicians. It is more difficult to produce economically in the United States, according to Kammüller. Labor costs are about 80 percent the German level, but it is difficult to find the workers that Trumpf needs, and Kammüller complained that the American operation still requires too much help from German expats. "There are simply too few engineers," Kammüller says. "It's difficult to find good people." Alas, that is not a very encouraging appraisal of America as a location for industry.

Of course, not every foreign company has such a positive experience in China. It is not a democratic country, and there is risk of arbitrary action by the government. Widespread official corruption can ensnare foreign executives, such as the finance manager for British drugmaker Glaxo-SmithKline, who was barred from leaving the country in 2013 amid a bribery probe. China remains a developing country, where it can be difficult to find local people able to maintain German standards of service and quality. Daimler, whose headquarters in Stuttgart is not far from Trumpf's base in the suburb of Ditzingen, struggled to establish an effective dealer network for Mercedes cars in China, and was not able to profit from the market as well as rivals BMW and Audi. While Chinese workers are efficient and reliable, Mathias Kammüller says, they are quick to jump ship if they get a better offer. "The money has to be right," Kammüller says. "If someone else pays them 20 percent more, they go." In Germany, Trumpf employee turnover is extremely low—1 percent or 2 percent a year—partly because Germans tend to feel close ties to their home region and are reluctant to move.

Protecting intellectual property is a constant challenge in China. Trumpf and other companies continue to keep their most valuable secrets close to home. In Trumpf's case, that means producing core components like lasers in Germany as well as the software and other technology used to control the cutting machines. Chinese companies have proven adept at copying Trumpf machines. Kammüller says the best way to deal with that problem is to remain innovative; the company invests about 8 percent of sales in research and development. "If they copy a machine, in two years we have a new one," he says. The real threat will come when Chinese companies learn to build machines that are as good as the German products and then to introduce innovations that give them a competitive advantage. "The Chinese machines are not as precise, or as high quality as European," Mathias Kammüller says, "but they are learning."

Despite the risks, there is little doubt that the investment in China paid off for Trumpf. After the collapse of Lehman Brothers in 2008 triggered a global financial crisis, sales of

Trumpf and many other German companies plummeted. Even by the standards of the machinery industry, with its extreme sensitivity to economic cycles, it was a grave crisis. Within two years, however, sales had rebounded at an amazing rate. In the fiscal year ended June 30, 2011, Trumpf sales shot up 50 percent, to more than 2 billion euros. The main reason was China.[6]

Plenty of other German companies can tell similar stories, not only about China but other emerging markets. "Our newest plants are in Russia, China, and India," Heinrich Weiss, chief executive of SMS Group, told me in 2011.[7] The company, based in Dusseldorf, builds and equips steel and aluminum plants. SMS spent 24 million euros on plane tickets in 2011, out of total sales of about 3 billion euros, Weiss said, mostly for travel to the developing world.

Another example is Multivac, based in Wolfertschwenden in southern Germany, which makes machines for packaging perishable goods. The company can only sell its products in countries where food can be kept cool from the farm to the factory to store shelves. So Multivac is something of an indicator of the advance of reliable electrical power and rising incomes. Hans-Joachim Boekstegers, the president of Multivac, told me he spent 150 days away from home in 2011 visiting fast-growing markets like Chile, Turkey, and Azerbaijan.[8]

German business people are not the only ones exploring the developing world, but one characteristic of the best German companies, even small ones, is their willingness to brave the risks and discomforts of foreign expansion. Berthold Leibinger was one such intrepid explorer of new markets when Trumpf was still a decidedly Mittelstand company, with sales well under $50 million a year. In the 1970s, when the Iron Curtain was still in place and the Cold War was still the fulcrum of international diplomacy, Leibinger even tried to find customers in the Eastern Bloc. After a particularly unpleasant night in a Moscow hotel, during which a broken toilet flushed continuously, Leibinger always made sure to carry a screwdriver and plumber's pliers with him. Another time, he was forced to trudge on foot along an icy road in the middle of the night to cover the several kilometers separating Czech and German border posts. His Czech driver could go no further than the checkpoint. (A motorist heading to Germany eventually came along and gave him a lift.) Leibinger never made many sales on that side of the Iron Curtain in those days, but such experiences helped prepare him and the company for future adventures in China and other emerging markets.

Some analysts and businesspersons warn that Germany is focusing too much on developing markets and setting itself up for a shock if China slows down. Germany's dependence on exports has grown as its traditional trading partners in Continental Europe have sunk into a prolonged torpor. China is clearly trying to build up its own expertise in autos and machinery, and become a competitor as well as a customer. Businesspersons are aware of the risk. But, said Nicola Leibinger-Kammüller, Berthold's daughter and successor as chief executive of Trumpf, "it is riskier not to be there."[9]

10

Cars, Engineers, and the Internet

If there is a living symbol of the revival of German industry, it may be Norbert Reithofer, the chief executive of BMW. In the 1980s, when he was a recent university graduate, and a junior professor of manufacturing science at a technical university in Munich, Reithofer wrote a book—still in print—that could serve as a manifesto for the German economy today.[1]

Reithofer argued that a country with little oil or other natural resources or innate geographical advantages had no other option but to automate ruthlessly, to become the most flexible and efficient country in the world. Reithofer, BMW's chief executive since 2006, has since put that principle to work in a way that has made the company the leading luxury car maker in the world, and one that is a pioneer in new technology such as battery-powered cars. BMW has remained profitable through several auto industry crises, becoming something of an icon of the revival of German industry.

BMW has factories all over the world, including in South Carolina and China. But it still makes 60 percent of its cars in Germany, about 1 million vehicles a year, and its heart remains in Bavaria. The BMW plant in Munich, next to the executive headquarters, is on the edge of downtown, adjacent to the expansive greenery of the city's Olympic Park, on some of the priciest real estate in Germany. The neighborhood was rural when BMW first began producing motors at the site in 1922, but it has long since been engulfed by the city. Nearby, apartments rent for several thousand euros a month.

A bean counter might advise BMW to move the factory elsewhere and sell the real estate. In fact, BMW has a global manufacturing network that it continues to expand, recently with a new plant in Brazil. And BMW managers have debated among themselves whether it really makes sense to build cars so close to downtown Munich. The company continues to do so in part because it has already invested untold billions in the site over the decades, which would be costly to replace. But there are other reasons that are harder to quantify but still real. It is BMW doctrine that executives, designers, and engineers should never be far from the factory floor—that all the expertise that goes into building an automobile cannot be too removed from the manufacturing process.

BMW has its share of bean counters, but the engineers are in charge, beginning with Reithofer. He was at the helm of production before becoming chief executive in 2006, and sees a close tie between manufacturing and development. "If you're not capable of being an industrial nation, then you're not capable of being a place to innovate," Reithofer told me in 2012 when I met him in BMW headquarters, a high-rise building shaped like four cylinders that, from the upper stories, has a clear view of the Bavarian Alps.[2]

Reithofer's view is at odds with the modern practice of companies like Apple that design products at headquarters, but leave production to contractors in Asia. At the same time, Reithofer, an ebullient man whose default facial expression is an amused smile, is an admirer of America. He attributes much of his business outlook to the three years, from 1997 to 2000, that he spent overseeing BMW's factory in Spartanburg, South Carolina. Soon after arriving, Mr. Reithofer recalled, he presented managers there with a list of problems. They corrected him. "Norbert," they said, according to Reithofer, "here in the United States we don't have problems. We have challenges. And every challenge is an opportunity."

That expression of American can-do spirit "left a deep, deep impression on me," Reithofer says. According to aides, Reithofer tells this story at least once a week. It is not at all unusual for German managers to praise their American counterparts, even as they ruthlessly beat them in the market. Like their predecessors in the nineteenth century, the best German companies ensure that their managers spend time abroad. The most open-minded of them, at least, do not operate on the assumption that Germany has a monopoly on management wisdom.

The proximity of the factory puts Reithofer almost literally next to the beating heart of the company. Just below the BMW executive offices is a building that houses a gigantic press that rhythmically stamps out side panels and other pieces of 3 Series sedans, the company's best-selling model. Despite heavy soundproofing, the building emits a steady, bass throbbing sound.

Proximity to the factory is standard for German carmakers, although none are quite as close to the center of a major city as BMW. Volkswagen's central headquarters overlooks the enormous production complex in Wolfsburg where Golf sedans and other models are made. Daimler's executives sit in the middle of a manufacturing operation near Stuttgart. For German auto executives, working within easy walking distance of the assembly line is *selbstverständlich*— something they take for granted.

Reithofer is not far from his customers, either. He can look down from the executive offices and see people taking delivery of new cars at BMW Welt—BMW World—the haute design structure where the company showcases all its brands, from Rolls-Royce to BMW motorcycles. Along with the BMW museum across the street, BMW Welt is a major tourist attraction, drawing more visitors per year than Neuschwanstein Castle, the fairytale palace southwest of Munich that was the inspiration for the castles at Disneyland. BMW Welt has several upscale restaurants and a large shop where visitors can buy BMW polo shirts or luggage, basking in the BMW brand even if they might not be able to afford a BMW vehicle. On one day that I visited, a young motorcycle stunt rider showed off on the polished exhibition floor of BMW Welt, popping wheelies or zooming up and down the wide staircases. The center of BMW's research and development (R&D) is located in a bustling low-rise office building a few blocks away.

The benefits of proximity are hard to quantify, but nonetheless real. "For developers, it's not bad to go into the factory and see what they built," says Jürgen Maidl, a BMW senior vice president in charge of network steering and logistics.[3] Maidl is one of the people in charge of making sure that BMW can produce efficiently at the Munich site. He is, in other words, responsible for applying the doctrine that Reithofer set out in his doctoral thesis many years ago. When Reithofer was studying, of course, computers were still a pretty new invention, and their deployment in German industry still a novelty. Now information technology (IT) is the key to producing successfully in Germany, and the integration of IT with manufacturing is where some German companies are arguably as revolutionary in their own way as any Silicon Valley start-up.

One of the first things that the thousands of tourists who tour the BMW factory every year notice is how few workers there are. Much of the assembly is done by robots, often supplied by another German company: Kuka, based in Augsburg, not far from Munich. In a glass chamber, for example, amazingly lifelike arms spray raw car bodies with paint. The robots are more precise than a person would be, waste less paint, and do not get sick from the fumes.

But it would be a mistake to see automation and IT merely as a way to replace human beings with uncomplaining, nonunionized robots. At BMW, IT is used to lower costs at the same time that it increases the company's ability to fulfill its customers' desires. That is ultimately good for jobs, especially in the auto industry, where the gravitational pull is toward emerging markets and away from mature, slow-growth markets like Europe.

These days, with the help of customized IT that BMW considers one of its competitive advantages, more than half of BMW buyers worldwide order cars with the precise selection of options that they want. They can choose the color of the exterior, leather or leatherette seats, manual or automatic transmission, and details like a heated steering wheel or a rearview camera. (In Germany, fussy buyers almost always want to design their own car. U.S. buyers, being more inclined to instant gratification, are more likely to buy a car off the lot.) With around 80 options on less expensive models like the 3 Series, and more than 100 on the top-of-the-line 7 Series, the possible combinations are almost endless. The surprising thing is that, having mastered the complexities of manufacturing cars to order, BMW actually saves money on manufacturing, while giving customers a product more closely aligned to their desires.

The process starts at BMW dealerships, where customers sit down with a dealer to configure their vehicle. Say you want a 528i sedan with imperial blue metallic exterior paint, ivory white nappa leather interior, satellite radio, moonroof, and night vision with pedestrian protection. Using an internal IT system designed by BMW, the dealer passes the information via the Internet to a central computer, which automatically notifies the corresponding parts suppliers. (Customers can also configure their dream car on the BMW website before even visiting a dealer.) The initial configuration is known as a prognosis. It is not yet a firm order—customers often change their minds and are allowed to do so. Rather, it is an alert to the entire components supply chain that certain parts may soon be needed.

At the same time, the system generates an estimate of how quickly the vehicle can be produced. The time can be as little as three weeks for a customer located not far from Spartanburg, South Carolina, where BMW produces primarily SUVs. The delivery time would be much longer for a car made in Germany that must traverse the Atlantic.

Customers are allowed to fiddle with their preferences for a while, but at a certain point the order is fixed. The system then calculates the best time to produce the vehicle—where in the manufacturing sequence it would fit most efficiently. The necessary parts are also ordered automatically. If the moonroof installation robot is off-line for maintenance, for example, the computer system will not schedule any cars with moonroofs until the maintenance work is done, and it will not order any moonroofs either.

As cars move through the factory, the elements of each customer-ordered car are already waiting, queued in sequence at the proper place in the production line, ready to be installed. Your satellite radio and night vision electronics will be waiting on a rack when your car reaches the appropriate assembly point. The worker or the robot, as the case may be, grabs the part and installs it. Each car carries a computer printout on the hood, which assembly line workers can check if there is any doubt about which part goes with which car.

The system does not always work perfectly. Sometimes the right part does not show up in the right sequence. But if that happens, the car is simply taken out of the assembly line until the problem can be corrected, without interrupting the overall flow. Or in some cases the part is added after the car has completed its trip through the assembly line.

The assembly lines, meanwhile, are built to handle a variety of cars. The BMW factory in Dingolfing, about 50 miles northeast of Munich, can produce 16 different models on its two assembly lines, ranging from variants of the 3 Series to underbodies for Rolls-Royce Phantoms. (Rolls-Royce belongs to BMW.) In the old days, assembly lines had to be reconfigured to produce variations of the same car. Today, it is not unusual to see different models, with different colors and different options, trailing each other through the factory in a kind of industrial conga line. The beauty of the system, from BMW's point of view, is that it is more efficient at the same time that it offers something that customers are willing to pay more for.

In the old days, BMW kept different types of parts in bins near the assembly line. Workers grabbed what they needed. With the new system, called just-in-sequence, BMW orders the parts it needs, in the order in which it needs them, as shortly as possible before it needs them. Maidl, the senior vice president in charge of the system, says that there is never more than two or three shifts worth of inventory at the factory. The savings from keeping parts inventory to a minimum are enormous. Consider that BMW buys on the order of 30 billion euros worth of components a year. If the company only needs to have 1 percent of that volume on its books at any one time, rather than 10 percent, the savings are in the billions. What the customer perceives is that he is getting exactly the color of leather seats that he or she wants, in addition to that built-in snowboard rack. "We are not doing this for the costs, we are doing it for the customer," says Maidl, an affable man with slightly unruly gray hair that makes him look like a professor at Hogwarts.

This is how the information revolution came to Germany. Like the Industrial Revolution a century earlier, it arrived late to Germany. Then it took hold with a vengeance, in a very German way. The country has yet to produce any Internet companies of global significance—that is, no web-based start-ups like Facebook that rocket from obscurity to global dominance in a matter of years, making their founders rich. The closest thing Germany has to offer are a few Internet-based businesses like Spreadshirt, which lets people design and order their own T-shirts over the Internet. It was a clever idea that has been a financial success, but it has not changed the world.

Germans did play a key role in founding some huge tech companies, including Google. But they typically did so from Silicon Valley, where there was creative energy and venture capital they could not find in Hamburg. As we have seen, Thomas Middelhoff's attempt to position Bertelsmann at the forefront of Internet innovation ended badly. The Neuer

Markt, Germany's answer to NASDAQ, and an attempt to encourage tech start-ups, performed so disastrously that it was forced to cease trading.

Germany's biggest contribution to the world of IT has been in the form of business-to-business software. The most notable example is SAP, based in Walldorf, Germany, the world's largest maker of so-called enterprise software. Software AG, in Darmstadt, is another example. SAP was founded before the Internet was in wide use, and has many customers in manufacturing. German managers like to make things. When they could use IT to produce goods better and more efficiently, it made sense to them.

In fact, labor costs account for less and less of the cost of producing a BMW. When German executives worry about labor, it is not so much the cost, but whether they can find enough engineers and other skilled people to operate the high-tech assembly lines. The integration of IT with factory engineering is already pervasive, but there remains huge potential for further efficiency. The balance of power could well shift from countries with low-cost workers to those with highly skilled workers able to manage complex manufacturing systems—if those countries can cultivate the right skills.

BMW, a sprawling multinational that is a household name around the world, is obviously in a different category than the small *Mittelstand* companies we have met in this book. Yet Reithofer has a lot in common with the stereotypical Mittelstand manager, and BMW is run along many of the same principles that characterize German mid-sized companies, albeit on a global scale.

Though he has a natural preference for data and rational analysis, Reithofer is another example of a German manager who is capable of going with his gut. Reithofer prefers to take a very methodical, analytical approach, Rainer Feurer, BMW's head of strategy, told me. But, Feurer added, "He is very courageous. He is ready to make risky decisions."[4]

In 2007, a large BMW dealer in the United States warned Reithofer that the subprime real estate crisis was beginning to hurt sales. Reithofer returned to Germany and persuaded the company's board of management to cut production even though evidence of a downturn was only anecdotal. "That was a very turbulent board meeting," Reithofer recalled. It took nerve to cut production when sales were still good. Although Reithofer, born in 1956, did not experience the war or the postwar privation, perhaps he absorbed some of the German ability to survive catastrophe. "In my experience," says Chris Bangle, former chief of design at BMW and now head of his own design firm based in a small town in northern Italy, "the top management of BMW have that stiff Prussian officer capability to stand fast under fire drilled into them from the cradle—even if they are Bavarian."[5]

Reithofer's decision to curtail production proved correct. In contrast to competitors like Daimler, to say nothing of the American automakers, BMW avoided any annual losses during the sharp recession that followed the collapse of Lehman Brothers in late 2008.

Reithofer says that another lesson he learned from the downturn in 2009 was that it pays to continue investing in future growth. Even as BMW cut production in 2009, it expanded its factory in Spartanburg and added a second factory in China. Similarly, even in the midst of the worst auto industry downturn Europe had seen in 20 years, BMW sharply increased spending on R&D, which increased by 15 percent in 2012 to about 3 billion euros.

Other German carmakers continued to invest as well. A survey by the consulting firm Ernst & Young in 2013 found that, despite the worst industry downturn in two decades, 40 percent of German car manufacturers said they planned to increase R&D and another 58 percent said that R&D spending would remain constant. Only 2 percent said they would cut research. For Europe as a whole, including Germany, 33 percent of carmakers said they would increase

R&D, and 60 percent said it would remain constant, with 7 percent expecting a decline. The German companies, in other words, were continuing to invest in innovation even in a crisis.[6]

The same survey also supported the idea that investment in R&D translates into innovation. Asked which country's auto industry was most innovative, 44 percent of the auto managers named Germany. Japan was second with 24 percent. The United States ranked fifth, behind South Korea and China, with 13 percent.

Much of BMW's R&D money went to support one of the most radical new initiatives by a major carmaker anywhere. In late 2013, BMW launched a battery-powered car, the i3, with a body made primarily of carbon fiber and aluminum. Those materials are substantially lighter than steel, but much more costly to employ in a mass-produced car. The decision to invest so much in the i project, which also included a plug-in hybrid four-seat sports car, was especially risky given that initial sales of pioneer electric cars like the Nissan Leaf or Chevy Volt were disappointing. There was little chance that the i3 would be profitable on a per-vehicle basis anytime soon, if ever. But Reithofer saw the so-called i3, a peppy four-seat city car built in Leipzig, as a way of preparing the company for long-term shifts in the industry.

The proposition that Germany is still a cost-effective location to build cars is certain to be tested in coming years. That may be especially true as BMW, as well as Daimler, moves into lower-priced market segments and becomes more and more a mass-market manufacturer. Daimler chose to build its B-Class small cars partly at a new factory in Hungary, where labor costs are substantially lower, but the workers are well trained.

The fortunes of BMW, Daimler, and Volkswagen have profound implications for all of Germany. Cars are Germany's largest export product, just ahead of machinery, and Germany's economic revival is due in no small part to demand from new markets, especially China. One of the risks Germany faces is its high dependence on the auto industry. Growth of auto sales in emerging markets will inevitably slow, and new competitors will emerge from China. Moreover, deep changes are underway in the automobile industry, which threaten to reshuffle the pecking order among carmakers, or even create openings for upstarts.

The price of fuel is only likely to rise in coming decades, forcing automakers to think about other means of propulsion. Governments are tightening fuel economy and emissions standards to the point where it will be difficult to manufacture the big luxury cars that generate the most profit per car for BMW and other manufacturers. Young people are increasingly apathetic about cars, which must compete with mobile phones and video games for their attention and money. Even in America, the proportion of young people who are not bothering to get driver's licenses is growing. Chris Bangle, the former design chief, argues that the industry must worry about the decline in what he calls "its lifeblood—customers who grow up caring about cars."

"Any look into the stats on issuance of driver's licenses and involvement in cars by the youth in U.S.A., Japan, and Europe shows this," Bangle says.

Reithofer is very aware of the risks. Carmakers must ensure that they are not blindsided by a technology shift, as has happened so often in the computer and software industries, he says. He does not want to become a Hewlett Packard, or a Nokia, a company that lost its dominance in its market because it reacted too slowly to a shift in technology— the iPhone and its touch screen interface. Reithofer was not reassured by the fact that it is difficult for a newcomer to break into the auto business. Much more than mobile phones or personal computers, automobile manufacturing requires a massive industrial base. Still, the Hyundai and Kia alliance of South Korea has shown that a determined newcomer with the right combination of price, performance, and design can become a major player. Hyundai and Kia were building market share and sales in Europe at the same time that European mass market brands like Peugeot or General Motors' Opel unit were compiling huge losses. Even California-based electric carmaker Tesla, despite epic start-up problems, showed that it was possible to begin from scratch in the auto industry (though it remains to be seen whether Tesla will be successful in the long run). The risk of overlooking the threat of new technology is especially great in a large and successful company like BMW, with more than 100,000 employees worldwide. Arrogance and complacency are a constant danger.

So far, at least, BMW has show flexibility in meeting such challenges. The company's investment in battery power or fuel-saving three-cylinder engines was in many ways a repudiation of a century of automobile development, a decisive shift away from the obsession with horsepower and internal combustion, especially for BMW with its brand identity based on acceleration and handling. Reithofer saw the i project as a way of signaling to the organization that the transformation to new forms of propulsion was real and had the passionate support of top management. "I have to get the message across to the organization—people, things are changing!" he said.

At the very least, the i3 was insurance against the possibility that BMW and other established carmakers would be ambushed by a company like Tesla or some Chinese upstart no one had heard of yet. And even if the i3 was a failure in the market, BMW would have acquired valuable expertise in building lightweight vehicles. The architecture is as radical as the drive train, featuring a carbon-fiber passenger compartment mounted atop an aluminum chassis. The i3, the city car that launched the series, is glued rather than welded together. It will pioneer a new way to build cars, potentially offering a payoff even if battery power is a flop on the market. "Innovations don't always work like they should," Chris Bangle says. "The CEO will have to be able to take the heat if the early returns are not favorable, and hold his course."

BMW may have been more able to take a more long-term view because it is essentially a family-owned company—another thing that makes it something of a giant Mittelstand company. About 47 percent of BMW shares are owned by the widow and children of Herbert Quandt, who acquired a majority in BMW in 1960 when it was close to bankruptcy, and oversaw its revival. The family ownership gives BMW some immunity from the demands of fund managers and bank analysts focused on short-term profit.

Reithofer in many ways personifies the ideal of a Mittelstand manager. He grew up in a Bavarian village south of Munich where his father was a factory worker. Reithofer is a tall man who commands authority, but he lacks the imperial presence of some of his rivals, notably Martin Winterkorn of Volkswagen, who has been seen strutting around auto shows trailing a large entourage. Ferdinand Dudenhöffer, a professor at the University of Duisburg-Essen in Germany and well-known industry analyst, describes Reithofer as "*bodenständig*"—down to earth. When Reithofer spoke at a conference that Dudenhöffer organized, the BMW chief arrived an hour early and traveled alone, Dudenhöffer recalls.[7]

Reithofer joined BMW in 1987, shortly after writing his thesis on manufacturing, part of his doctoral work at the Technical University of Munich (where, as a student, he drove a used BMW). He required only 13 years to advance to the executive board, the top level of management.

Reithofer came up through the organization largely by way of the production floor, a logical progression for someone so steeped in engineering. But if you ask Reithofer what is the most important selling point for a BMW vehicle, his answer is surprising. The most important selling point is not the engine or the suspension, but rather the design—the aesthetics, Reithofer says. In that crucial area, the company has a history of hiring non-Germans as directors of design, notably Bangle, an American who spent 17 years at BMW before leaving in 2009. His successor, Adrian Van Hooydonk, is Dutch. So Reithofer embodies another characteristic of the ideal German manager. He is an engineer, but able to see problems from other points of view.

There is, in fact, no inherent conflict between design and engineering. Even if there are often disagreements between the two departments, the final product would not be beautiful if it were not also beautifully engineered. Though he has no formal design training, Reithofer would not have been as successful as he has been without an innate ability to critique prototypes on the basis of aesthetics. At least once a month, the entire BMW executive board reviews designs that are under development. BMW also holds design clinics with consumers, a kind of focus group in which prospective customers are asked to give their opinions on particular designs. Unlike engineering with its mathematical certainties, however, design is ultimately a subjective process that cannot be reduced to science. "It's a gut feeling," Reithofer says. "Does it speak to me or does it not speak to me?"

The ultimate expression of the merger of design and engineering may be the BMW factory in Leipzig, its newest German plant, which began turning out 1 Series cars in 2005. It is also where BMW is building the i3. BMW commissioned architect Zaha Hadid to design the delta-wing shaped office building that connects the production areas. To Reithofer and his breed of German manager, a factory is a beautiful thing.

11

Azubis and the Skills Pipeline

"Help wanted" signs are ubiquitous in the shop windows of the old town of Ingolstadt, a former garrison city for the Bavarian army—when Bavaria still had its own army—that is still largely surrounded by thick stone embattlements. A manufacturing city of 128,000 people on the banks of the Danube between Nuremburg and Munich, Ingolstadt provides an extreme example of the human dividend from Germany's renaissance—the rebound in the German job market that has occurred since the overhaul of labor regulations in 2005. After all, perhaps the ultimate measure of a national economy is its ability to generate jobs. Ingolstadt is also a proving ground for the German system for integrating young people into the workforce.

In 2012, unemployment in Ingolstadt and the surrounding region was just 2.2 percent, the lowest of any labor district in the country, and down from almost 10 percent a decade earlier. In Eichstätt, a neighboring town that is part of the district, the jobless rate was an almost impossibly low 1.3 percent. When unemployment is that low, the main problem for companies and local officials is not finding jobs for unemployed workers. The main problem is finding workers for unfilled jobs.

At one café I stopped at during a visit in 2012, there were two large chalkboards set up on the cobbled street in front. One advertised the lunch special (meat with gravy and a small salad), and the other sought counter help. It was tough to find workers and tough to keep them, the owner told me. "They're students. They go after a while," she said, before shooing me away because she was too busy to talk.[1]

There are two main reasons for the exceptionally low unemployment in Ingolstadt. One is the restructuring of the German labor market. The other is Audi, the luxury car unit of Volkswagen, which has its headquarters and one of its main factories in Ingolstadt. There may also be a third reason: China. Audi, the largest employer in the region, is booming because of exports to China as well as growing sales in North America. Ingolstadt is also lucky to have several other large employers in the region, including EADS, the aerospace conglomerate that has a plant nearby, and Osram, the lighting division of Siemens. Between them, they support a dense network of smaller components suppliers and service providers.

The *Mittelstand* companies in and around Ingolstadt are grateful for the business they get from Audi, of course. But they also struggle to compete with Audi for workers. Even young people, traditionally the hardest group to employ, are in high demand. "None of my friends have any problem getting a job," one 18-year-old woman, named Rebecca, told me. That is a statement you would not hear in Greece or Spain, where youth unemployment was well above 50 percent in 2013.

Germany's young people are beneficiaries of the country's centuries-old apprenticeship system. In its modern form, the system combines classroom education in a traditional high school or technical college with work experience and on-the-job training at an employer. The Germans refer to it as the "dual system." The apprentices are known as *Auszubildende*, the "to-be-trained," or *Azubis*, for short. The system, versions of which also exist in other countries like Austria and Switzerland (which also have low youth unemployment rates), has attracted increasing attention from abroad because of its success at directing young people who are not bound for university into skilled work.

I met Rebecca at Schabmüller Automobiltechnik, which makes components for Audi and other vehicle manufacturers. A striking blonde, she was learning how to use a metal lathe. (We took her picture for an article in the *New York Times*. When my editor saw the images, he commented, "What a country! They have fashion models working in the factories!") Schabmüller works hard to keep young people like Rebecca and another apprentice I met, a 21-year-old named Patrick. He weighed three offers before choosing Schabmüller.

The company, which in 2012 was operating around the clock seven days a week to keep up with demand, virtually promised Patrick a full-time job when he completed a machinists' training program. Patrick, who planned to divide his time between the Schabmüller factory and studies at a technical college, said he turned down an offer from Audi, considered by many people to be the premier employer. "At Audi I would be standing on the assembly line," he said, taking a break from practicing with a computer-controlled lathe. "Here there's more variety."

Making sure that enough young people share those sentiments has become a big worry for Franz Schabmüller, a local entrepreneur who owns Schabmüller Automobiltechnik, as well as a collection of other mid-sized companies in Bavaria. His other holdings include a company that produces motor components for BMW and a marble quarry. Schabmüller met me on a sunny September day at the headquarters of FS Firmenverwaltung, the umbrella company of his mini conglomerate, which is located in a residential neighborhood in Ingolstadt. We sat in plastic lawn furniture on a patio outside the modest company headquarters, where Schabmüller, a jovial man in his late 50s who was dressed informally in a blue shirt and jeans, smoked Marlboros and reminisced about a motorcycle trip he made across the United States in 2004 in which he retraced the route described by Robert Pirsig in his classic *Zen and the Art of Motorcycle Maintenance*. (Schabmüller's interest in both philosophy and auto parts might not be as odd as it seems. As a young man, Schabmüller studied theology at the University of Regensburg with a professor named Joseph Ratzinger, who later became the Pope.)

Though business was booming, Schabmüller was worried about finding enough qualified workers. Germany, he pointed out, was an aging society with a low birth rate and a shrinking supply of young people. "That's a long-term process that can't be stopped right away," he said. "The question for the Mittelstand is, what do you do about it?"[2]

The answer, for Schabmüller and many other mid-sized companies, is to exploit Germany's apprenticeship tradition. A few years back, there was an oversupply of young people looking for apprenticeships. But now, Ingolstadt employers must fight for competent young people. Schabmüller starts trying to win them over early. He and his managers set up booths at job fairs, and they speak at local schools on topics such as what a machinist does and why subjects like geometry are important in the real world. Schabmüller and company managers like Christian Stöhr, whose responsibilities include recruiting trainees for Schabmüller Automobiltechnik, try to stay on good terms with local teachers, in hopes that they will encourage their students to apply. "The mentality of young people has changed," says Stöhr. "They don't look for apprenticeships as actively as they used to. You have to go to them."[3]

The scarcity of reliable and motivated trainees has encouraged employers to reach outside the usual pool of young men. Schabmüller has been trying to attract more young women. Not only can they do the jobs just as well or better, but their presence helps motivate the lads, Franz Schabmüller maintains. "The boys try harder during training" when a woman is watching, he says.

Money also pays a role in attracting and keeping apprentices. Schabmüller was paying its Azubis 510 euros a month the first year (about $660 at the exchange rate in mid-2013), plus a 150 euro bonus if they maintained a B average or better. That is a decent wage considering that Azubis typically cost an employer far more than the value of any work they do. Much of what Azubis produce at Schabmüller is solely for practice. Among numerous Azubi projects on display at the entrance of Schabmüller Automobiltechnik was a chess set machined from steel. But some projects are pretty sophisticated. Schabmüller Azubis helped build a motorcycle modified to carry three people. Franz Schabmüller wants the trainees to feel a sense of pride, "so they can tell their aunt or their friends, 'I helped build that.'"

Once accepted into a training program, the Azubis alternate weeks at the factory with weeks in school. The proportion of workplace time to school time increases the closer they get to graduation. The programs that students undergo are subject to rigid requirements designed to ensure that the young people emerge with marketable skills and are not just exploited as cheap labor. There are roughly 350 approved programs,[4] ranging from cook or hairdresser to video editor or automobile industry quality management auditor. The system reflects the German obsession with training and titles, and also the tendency to try to codify education. Even house painters and florists undergo rigorous apprenticeships and qualification programs to earn the right to call themselves a *Meister.*

But apprenticeships have also become more and more sophisticated as demand has increased for specialized technical skills. Once trainees were typically teenagers, but now they are often students at technical colleges studying demanding specialties like mechatronics, the design and operation of systems that combine electronics and mechanical engineering. Mechatronics is becoming an increasingly important discipline at German automakers because of the growth of plug-in hybrid cars and the introduction of the first cars powered solely by batteries, like the BMW i Series.

The German apprenticeship system does a good job of absorbing those young people who lack the inclination or ability for university study. A person who has completed an *Ausbildung* in industrial machinery maintenance—who has become a Meister—enjoys a certain respect on the factory floor. Though he or she may not have attended college, his or her status is much higher than that of a simple high school graduate in the United States, and his or her pay may well be, too. "There are people who are cognitively a bit weaker but fabulous with their hands," says Jürgen Maidl, the senior vice president at BMW in charge of managing the company's logistics network we met earlier in this book.

The German system acknowledges that reading Goethe or learning Latin may not be very relevant for some youngsters. Rather than letting them drift or even drop out, the young people are encouraged to do something that corresponds to their skills. Christian, a young man to whom I spoke in 2009, gave up full-time schooling at age 15—normally not a very smart career move. But Christian, who lives in the German village of Ketsch, outside Heidelberg, became an apprentice at Helmut Herbert, a large plumbing contractor in nearby Bensheim. He alternated two weeks of on-the-job training with one week of classes at a vocational school. Christian was 18 when I spoke to him and getting ready to qualify in what were traditionally separate trades: heating, plumbing, and air-conditioning. He was clearly proud of his accomplishment. "You used to have to call three technicians. Now you only need one," he said.[5]

The system has its negative aspects. German children are typically divided up academically following the fourth grade. The brighter ones go to a Gymnasium, the gateway to a university education. The rest go to a *Realschule* or other less demanding school, which is likely to lead to vocational training and an apprenticeship. By about 10 years old, a young German's path in life is largely ordained.

The system can also be inflexible. Once a person is trained in a specialty, it can be difficult to switch. The older a worker becomes, the more difficult it becomes to change professions, which is a problem for anyone whose specialty becomes obsolete. The rigidity of professional qualification is one possible reason why older Germans are at greater risk of sinking into long-term unemployment than younger workers.[6] Because the training programs and examinations for professions like plumber or house painter are controlled by professional associations, there is also a risk that the qualification system can become a kind of cartel. By setting tough qualification requirements and insisting on long periods of apprenticeship, professional associations raise barriers to entry and limit competition.

Training young people is not a very profitable business, either, at least in the short run. Siemens spends several hundred million euros a year training Azubis. The company estimates that the productive work done by the trainees equals only about one-third their cost. Siemens, which offers almost all its apprentices full-time jobs, recoups the investment only later. German companies are not formally compelled to host Azubis, but it is considered a duty to do so and many companies find that it is in their interests. At times, patriotism has not been enough. The number of training slots declined 10 percent between 2000 and 2005, rising again only after the government threatened to make it mandatory for companies to take a certain number of Azubis.[7]

Those problems notwithstanding, the system is good at finding a place in society for those young people who may not be star students but have other talents. The system is also a good way for companies to train exactly the workers they need. "It's very good for the young people and not necessarily bad for us," Christian Stöhr at Schabmüller says.

Martin Kannegiesser, the maker of equipment for commercial laundries we met a few chapters earlier, says he hires Azubis whose fathers or even grandfathers have worked for the company. Kannegiesser says he treasures the sense of loyalty, which he believes is the company's reward for being a reliable employer. "Since the beginning of the company, we always had apprentices," Kannegiesser told me. "We employed them, we never sent them home when they finished their apprenticeships, in good times and in bad times."

"A tradition has developed," Kannegiesser said. "The last time I looked at the list of the new apprentices, I said, oh,

I know this name, I know this name—I know these names. They are people in the second or third generation already."

Once a company has trained a worker, it is loath to let him or her go. As a result, recent economic shocks have had little affect on the unemployment rate. When the global financial crisis hit in 2008, sales at Schabmüller's companies plunged, but he held onto his workers. Many other companies did the same. "As a rule I don't want to lose people—I have invested a lot in training," Franz Schabmüller says. The German government played a role by making it easier for companies to retain their employees during slumps. The program is known as *Kurzarbeit*, or "short work." Companies reduce the hours of surplus workers and the government helps make up for the lost pay. In most cases the cost to the government was less than paying unemployment benefits, and it meant that companies were able to respond quickly when global demand recovered strongly in late 2009. Government funds also allowed workers to use their idle time for training, so when the economy recovered they had more skills.

Ingolstadt was not always so prosperous. It was once regarded as a somewhat blighted corner of Bavaria. Author Mary Shelley set her novel *Frankenstein* partly in Ingolstadt, until recently one of the city's only claims to fame. The fictional Dr. Frankenstein attended medical school in Ingolstadt and stitched together a monster from body parts he scavenged from local graveyards. In modern Ingolstadt, the Frankenstein monster probably would not have had much trouble finding a job.

As recently as 2005, the jobless rate in Ingolstadt was more than 7 percent, three times the current level. Full employment is not necessarily the same as affluence, however. Ingolstadt remains a working-class community with none of the opulence of Munich to the south. Many neighborhoods consist of slab-like concrete apartment blocks, where the predominant language is often Turkish or Russian.

Ingolstadt has a historic city center surrounded by old fortress walls, but there are several empty storefronts.

As in Germany as a whole, the plunge in joblessness began with Chancellor Gerhard Schröder's reforms in 2005, which cut unemployment nationwide almost in half. This job miracle is regarded with curious ambivalence by many Germans, however. It came at the expense of the comfortable but costly social benefits many Germans treasured. People had to give up the security of a guaranteed long-term income if they became unemployed. They faced more pressure to take jobs they did not want. Many of the new jobs created since the reforms pay low wages, one reason why the changes in labor rules are still resented by many Germans. Even better-paid workers had to make do with meager pay raises. Labor costs in Germany barely budged during the first decade of the 2000s.

The wage restraint helped German companies become more competitive on world markets, and it helped prevent the loss of manufacturing jobs to Eastern Europe or China. But it also created a bigger gap between rich and poor. As already noted, Schröder pushed through the changes in labor rules in the face of bitter opposition within his own center-left party. He subsequently lost a reelection bid to Angela Merkel and has become a figure of some ridicule because of his business ties to Russian President Vladimir V. Putin. Schröder's fate has not been lost on subsequent generations of German politicians, or politicians in other European countries like France, who have not shown a lot of enthusiasm for continued reform of labor rules. Such changes are unpopular and typically take years to bear fruit, by which time the officials responsible have been kicked out of office.

Despite the 2005 reforms, most German workers continue to enjoy far more protections than those in the United States. Permanent workers can be dismissed for economic reasons only after lengthy negotiations with employers that

typically include hefty severance payments. German politicians remain reluctant to tamper with these legal barriers
to dismissal. As a result, temporary workers bear the brunt
of fluctuations in demand for labor, and allow companies
to quickly cut personnel costs in the event of a downturn.
"Flexibility in production is essential, and temporary workers definitely play a role," said Janina Kugel, who when I
spoke to her in 2012 was director of human resources and
executive development at Osram, the lighting division of
Siemens (since spun off in an initial public offering), which
has a factory in nearby Eichstätt.[8]

Temporary workers are formally employed by staffing
companies. They can be released in an instant from their
temporary employers. "Temporary work has boomed, but
there is a high degree of insecurity," Rolf Zöllner, head of the
Federal Labor Agency in Ingolstadt, told me. Staffing agen-
cies accounted for about 40 percent of the positions offered
through the labor agency in 2012.[9]

Labor leaders argue that Ingolstadt's full employment has
more to do with exports than reforms, and there is some
truth to that assertion. The job boom in Germany came at
the same time that China emerged as a huge market—in fact
the largest market for Volkswagen, Audi's parent company.
The effects of government policy are often difficult to disen-
tangle from the results of sound corporate strategy. "It's hard
to say, because the economy recovered at the same time,"
said Thomas Sigi, a member of the management board at
Audi who is in charge of personnel, "German industry prepared itself at the right time for emerging markets."[10]

But it is clear that Ingolstadt's success would not have been
possible without a trained workforce, and that the German
apprenticeship system played a role. Could America also
breed Azubis? Some German companies are already trying.
Stihl, the maker of chain saws, as well as Volkswagen, Bosch
and Siemens have established apprenticeship programs in
the United States. Typically, the apprentices are older, and

the classroom training takes place at a local community college during the evenings.[11] But those companies show that it can be done.

At its plant in Spartanburg, South Carolina, BMW trains workers in specialties like manufacturing machine maintenance. Graduates receive a diploma of sorts showing they are "BMW Certified." But Jürgen Maidl of BMW clearly longs for the German system, which more closely integrates public education with the private sector and puts young people on a vocational track at an earlier age. A young person who has completed training in machine maintenance is more likely to feel ownership of his machine and show initiative in solving and anticipating problems, Maidl says. And a state certified diploma in, say, applied mechatronics would be more valuable to an employee than a piece of paper recognized only within BMW, he says.

The U.S. educational system has the advantage of preparing more students for college, and it does not segregate the college bound from everyone else at a young age—at least not formally. (Obviously, there are big differences in the quality of American public high schools, often related to the affluence of the surrounding community and local taxpayers' willingness to finance education.) On the whole, the U.S. system offers students more second chances and does not penalize late bloomers as severely as the German system. Perhaps as a result, a larger percentage of young Americans than young Germans go on to college and earn degrees.[12] High school graduation rates in Germany and the United States are about the same, although there is evidence that German students leave school with higher proficiency in math and science.[13] But a comparison of youth unemployment rates—probably the ultimate indicator of how well a society prepares its young people for the job market—suggests that the German system is better at exploiting the potential of young people who may not get fabulous grades, but nonetheless have marketable talents. In 2012, the number of people under age 25 considered unemployed was 8.1 percent in Germany and 16.2 percent in the United States, according to Eurostat, the European Union statistics agency.[14] In Spain, where more than half of young people were unemployed as a result of that country's debt and economic crisis, there were efforts to adapt the German system for local use.

Berthold Leibinger of Trumpf, who knows America well, even suggested that the American obsession with a college education has gone too far. For generations of immigrants, he pointed out, sending a child to college was fulfillment of the American dream. He recalled German emigrants he met while working in Ohio in the 1950s. "They all had one wish—my Johnny has to go to college. Skilled workers in Germany should have a higher status than they do, but it's still respectable," he said.

The point may not be which system is better, but what the two countries could learn from each other. There is no reason why American states or communities could not establish their own versions of the German apprenticeship system. America has a long tradition of internships. At institutions of higher learning like Northeastern University in Boston, work experience is a required part of the path students take to earning a diploma. On-the-job experience would be more valuable if it were linked institutionally to education, so that young people could make progress toward diplomas while spending substantial amounts of their time at an employer. That would require a greater commitment both from school systems and companies. Firms would have to ensure that interns are not just running errands, but rather learning something useful. Schools would have to orient classwork more closely to the needs of local firms. Young people, too, must make more of a commitment than many are accustomed to by American traditions and culture.

While Ingolstadt is a shining example of the success of German job policy, it also may illustrate the lingering vulnerabilities of the German economy. Some people in town wonder what would happen if Audi, still booming in 2013, ever suffered a slump in sales. The carmaker employs 35,000 people in Ingolstadt, not counting the people who work for suppliers like Schabmüller.

With China's economy wobbling in 2013, the German economy slowing, and mass-market carmakers in Europe suffering from ruinous excess factory capacity, some people worried that the boom in Ingolstadt could fade. "We are very concerned about what would happen if Audi had a sales problem," said Bernhard Stiedl, deputy head of the IG Metall union in Ingolstadt, which represents Audi workers. "It would have a massive effect on us."[15]

As a society, Germany is aging, and companies face a dwindling supply of young workers. As successful as it is, the German educational system must remain adaptable so that it can meet the changing needs of young people and, most importantly, those of industry. "A growing shortage of highly qualified personnel is likely in the coming years because of ongoing technological changes and population ageing," the Organization for Economic Cooperation and Development warned in a 2013 study.[16]

Karl-Heinz Paqué, a well-known German economist, even argues that Germany is on its way to becoming a full-employment society, where the kind of labor shortages seen in Ingolstadt are pervasive nationwide. The German baby boomer generation will retire between 2020 and 2035, creating a huge skills shortage, predicts Paqué, a professor at the University of Magdeburg. "The labor market will become a seller's market rather than a buyer's market," he argued in the pages of the *Frankfurter Allgemeine* newspaper in 2013.[17] Full employment is mostly a good thing, and will encourage employers to train less qualified people while discouraging them from making job cutbacks during downturns. When sales recover, companies know they could face problems finding qualified people again. But

Paqué warns that very low unemployment rates such as those already prevalent in Bavaria could lead policymakers to forget how joblessness fell so low in the first place. Labor unions will be tempted to seek wage increases not justified by higher productivity, while politicians may reintroduce excessive labor regulation. "A feeling of approaching full employment can quickly lead to overconfidence," wrote Paqué, who knows something about politics. He was a member of the state Parliament in Saxony Anhalt and for a while served as the state finance minister. Germany's success at creating jobs—which has put more people to work than the Bismarck era—could, he wrote, cause Germans "to lose sight of the original source of progress."

For now, Ingolstadt has problems many cities would envy. While many communities are suffering from declining population because of low birthrates, Ingolstadt is adding 1,000 residents a year, and construction companies are busy putting up housing. Financially strapped cities elsewhere are closing schools and public swimming pools; Ingolstadt is building new ones. Audi has sponsored new sports stadiums and professional soccer and hockey teams.

The job market has even vacuumed up people that used to be considered unemployable. After the collapse of the Soviet Union, Ingolstadt was a destination for many ethnic Germans in places like Kazakhstan that, under German law, had a right to citizenship. But many did not speak German or have marketable skills, and were blamed for a rise in crime. That problem has all but disappeared, says Herbert Lorenz, head of the Ingolstadt economic development office. "The best social policy," he said, "is full employment."[18]

12

The Education of a German Manager

In a rare extravagance a few years ago, Dagmar Bollin-Flade and her husband, Bernd Flade, commissioned an artist to make an Andy Warhol-style print of one of their high-end plumbing fixtures. They were pleased with the results, except that the artist framed the work crookedly. After trying unsuccessfully to open the frame and straighten the print, Dagmar and Bernd telephoned the artist, who explained that she had intended the image to hang at a slight angle, for aesthetic effect. Dagmar and Bernd laugh when they tell the story now, but at the time they could not fathom why anyone would make a picture crooked. They are engineers. A crooked print violated everything they ever learned about precision and order. Later, at a trade fair, they hung the image at the Bollin Armaturenfabrik stand. To their amusement, one engineer after another approached them to point out that the print was very nice, but it was crooked.

The German engineering mentality has its roots in tradition, but it is sustained by education. German technical colleges and universities awarded about 65,000 degrees in engineering, manufacturing, and construction in 2011,[1] compared to about 83,000 people who earned engineering degrees in the United States.[2] Even adjusting for differences in the way the professions are classified and the length of time it takes to earn a degree in each country, it is clear that Germany is producing far more engineers on a per capita basis than the United States. According to United Nations Educational, Scientific, and Cultural Organization (UNESCO) figures from 2010, 7.2 percent of U.S. students in postsecondary education were pursuing degrees in engineering, construction, and manufacturing. In Germany, the figure was 16.4 percent.[3] (At 24.9 percent, Finland was the world champion in producing engineers, and was also rated the most competitive country in Europe by the World Economic Forum.)[4]

What is more, the number of engineers graduating from German universities is growing. The profession suffered a slump between 1995 and 2005, with the number of engineering graduates falling by nearly one-quarter. But since then, in response to heavy demand, the number of engineering graduates has rebounded, rising 17 percent in 2011 compared to the year before. The growth rate for engineering grads in the United States during the same time period was 5.6 percent.

The United States, on the other hand, is the capital of the MBA. About 100,000 people in the United States earned master's degrees in business administration in 2011, in addition to roughly another 50,000 who earned other kinds of graduate business degrees.[5] Business is also a popular course of study in Germany, however. According to the UNESCO figures (considered the most reliable cross-national statistics on higher education), 26.2 percent of German students were pursuing degrees in social sciences, business, or law, almost as high as the United States with 27.7 percent. In Germany, the traditional course of business study is known as *Betriebswirtschaftslehre*, and can be part of a four-year bachelor's program or a six-year program leading to a master's degree. MBAs on the American model, attended by students who already have a university degree and usually a few years of work experience, are offered by institutions like the University of Mannheim and are growing in popularity.

Who is better at the top of a manufacturing company, an MBA or a *Diplom-Ingeniuer*? German managers' answer to that question is pretty clear. "You have to be an engineer," says Norbert Reithofer of BMW. The business of designing and building automobiles is just too complex for a non-engineer to master, he maintains. That belief prevails at the other German carmakers as well. Martin Winterkorn, the head of Volkswagen, has a doctorate in metallurgy that he earned at the prestigious Max Planck Institute for Metal Research.[6] Dieter Zetsche, chief executive of Daimler, has a doctorate in engineering from the University of Paderborn.[7]

At least in recent history, American car companies have not done very well when they put marketing or finance specialists in charge. Ford had Jacques Nasser, and Chrysler had Robert Nardelli. Rick Wagoner's Harvard MBA may have helped him reach the top of General Motors, but it was not enough to allow him to turn the company around. Whether or not these three managers bear the blame for the decline of the U.S. automobile industry in the 2000s, at the very least their tenures coincided with unhappy times. It may just be a coincidence, but the revival of the Big Three came after the appointment of managers with at least some, and some cases a lot of, training as engineers: Alan Mulally of Ford, Daniel Akerson of General Motors, and Sergio Marchionne of Chrysler.

To the German way of thinking, the engineers should lead and other disciplines should follow. Ferdinand Piëch, a scion of the Porsche family who later led a turnaround at Volkswagen, was dismissive of competitors who do it any other way. Without mentioning Toyota or General Motors by name, Piëch, who later became chairman of the supervisory board of Volkswagen, told a German auto magazine in 2013: "One or two competitors are still ahead of us, but they tick much differently. One has a very austere multibrand strategy. The other borrowed a lot of capital from the American government. Both are managed more commercially than we are. In our company, the engineer develops a component and gives it to the chief buyer, who is supposed to negotiate a good price with the supplier. At one, if not both, of our competitors, the price is set first, and then the poor engineer has to design a part that under no circumstances may cost any more. That is by definition not as close to the customer."[8]

Piëch's point is that the first priority should be to make a beautifully engineered car; everything else is subservient. Obviously, finance and marketing have their place, but they are secondary to the primary mission, product excellence. It takes an engineer to enforce the standards of perfectionism that make "Made in Germany" such an enduring brand.

But it is also clear that being a brilliant engineer is not enough for an individual to lead a successful company. Managers may fail if they are not also able to lead and inspire their people, understand the nuances of finance, and be good salespeople. Though he spent much of his career managing factories, Norbert Reithofer of BMW is a natural showman able to play the stage impresario when launching a new model at an auto show. (Dieter Zetsche of Daimler is another engineer with theatrical skills.) Reithofer, as we have already discussed, also has a keen appreciation for the aesthetics of an automobile, and says that design, not engineering, is the most important factor in a customer's decision to buy a BMW. The company does plenty of market research about what designs most appeal to customers, but the final decision about what prototypes to produce is a matter of gut feeling, Reithofer says. He is an engineer, yes, but also able to act on intuition, as he did when deciding to slash production ahead of the 2009 downturn even though hard evidence of a recession was thin.

How does an engineer become more than an engineer? Berthold Leibinger of Trumpf argues that engineers should take care to learn about art and culture, to broaden their minds beyond the mathematical certainties of their métier. His own studies in mechanical engineering were "demanding but not inspiring," Trump wrote in his memoirs. "The German education for engineers is good, but it lacks something. To this day, engineers who train other engineers have failed to understand that. Their students have to guide and manage other people later in life—but they hear nothing from their teachers about just how they should do it. The achievements of engineers are changing the world, yet at the technical universities one learns next to nothing about that world, or the condition it is in."[9] Leibinger filled in those gaps himself, in particular by traveling to America as a young man.

It is certainly possible for non-engineers to be successful managers of manufacturing companies. Martin Kannegiesser, the son of an engineer, studied business economics at the University of Cologne and was phenomenally successful both in expanding the family laundry machinery business and as a leader of his industry. After serving as president of Gesamtmetall, the car and metal industry employers association, Kannegiesser became president of the European umbrella organization for the industry, known as CEEMET. Isabel Hahn of Glasbau Hahn also studied business economics, although she expressed some regret to me that she did not have an engineering degree. She compensated by marrying someone who had a degree in machinery construction; he also works for Glasbau Hahn.

There is evidence that a country's economic success actually depends not just on technical and scientific competence but on a workforce educated in a range of skills, including humanities. Günther Rehme, an economist at the Technical University of Darmstadt, analyzed the UNESCO data in depth, looking for correlations between economic growth and the types of university graduates a country produced. The surprising conclusion: "All subject areas were associated positively with growth." People who studied humanities—literature, history, ancient Greek, and so forth—appear to complement the engineers and physicists, at least at a macroeconomic level.[10]

The choice between engineering and business education need not be an either/or proposition. Increasingly, German educational institutions are attempting to give people with technical degrees an alternative to the self-education that was the only way for many in Leibinger's generation to broaden their horizons. For more than a century it has been possible to study to be a *Wirtschaftsingenieur*, an economist-engineer with expertise in both disciplines. But the program was offered at relatively few universities until recent decades, when it has experienced a boom in popularity. And there remains the quandary of the young person who studies engineering expecting to spend his or her career designing the perfect transmission, only to find himself or herself promoted to a supervisory position later in life. For a person accustomed to the certainties of math and physics, managing human beings with all their imperfections can be a rude shock.

One solution can be found in an unlikely location not far from Unter den Linden, the boulevard that marches down the historic center of Berlin. In 2002, several dozen of Germany's largest corporations, including BMW, Siemens, and Daimler, donated the money used to found the European School of Management Technology, or ESMT, in an effort to improve the quality of business education in Germany. One focus is teaching management skills to engineers or other people who studied technical disciplines as undergraduates. ESMT occupies a sprawling building close to the River Spree that once housed the administrative offices of the East German Communist regime. It is a rather ironic setting for a school devoted to the principles of free-market capitalism. The building, the size of a city block, is an imposing example of postwar socialist architecture, with high ceilings and oversized corridors designed to make people feel small and impress them with the power of the state. The current occupants have done their best to make the atmosphere friendlier. A vast office once used by Erich Honecker, the last ruler of East Germany, has been converted to a lounge and coffee bar.

For people at the beginning of their careers, with an undergraduate degree and a few years of work experience, ESMT offers a 12-month master's of business administration along American lines, but with an emphasis on training managers in technology and manufacturing companies. Jörg Rocholl, a banking expert who is the school's energetic president, says that between 35 percent and 50 percent of an average entering class consists of people who have previously studied engineering. The overwhelming majority of students go into manufacturing or technology companies after they graduate. "We have very few graduates, almost none, who go into investment banking," Rocholl says. Rocholl notes the contrast with Columbia University in New York, where he earned his doctorate and where investment banks used to sponsor happy hours for MBA students and vacuum them up after graduation. "I don't know if there was one person in manufacturing," Rocholl says.[11]

ESMT also has part-time programs for engineers or other specialists who are well into their careers and find themselves trying to learn about things that were not on the curriculum at the technical university, like marketing, negotiation, or human resources. And the school offers custom part-time programs for companies wanting to upgrade the skills of their own managers.

How do you teach an engineer to deal with squishy, inexact topics like psychology and group decision-making? It is not always easy. "Engineers have high aspirations," says Christoph Burger, who is in charge of setting up customized programs at ESMT. "They want to know what is true. In business administration you can't say if it's true. You deal with probabilities."[12]

In his courses, Burger, who teaches decision-making, often uses a hypothetical case study that illustrates the perils of approaching problems with too much of an engineering mindset. The case concerns managers of a second-tier auto racing team who have a chance to enter a major event. The race could be their entrée to the big leagues and more sponsorship dollars. But though the team has often finished well in past lower-level races, its engines have a tendency to fail in spectacular and dangerous fashion. If the team decides to enter a major race and the engine explodes, it would be a costly failure that could lead to loss of existing sponsors and ruin the company. Further complicating the decision, it is not clear why the engines are blowing up.[13]

For engineers, who break into groups to decide what to do, the case is a bit of a trap. They tend to argue that management is about taking risk, especially in the car racing industry. Thus, the majority decides to enter the race, Burger says. "They just see the win and the new money and off they go," Burger says. That is not necessarily the right decision. At the very least, students in the program should agree whether the probability of failure is acceptable or too high.

Engineers often have trouble dealing with business risk, Burger says. As engineers they are supposed to minimize risk, to make sure that machines operate exactly as they are supposed to and not fail. That training in risk aversion can put them at a disadvantage when confronting a problem of company strategy, where the outcomes are harder to predict. Sometimes engineers, aware that they are naturally risk averse, overcompensate and become too reckless. Burger uses the auto racing case to point out the perils of hubris as well as the hazards of group decision-making. Managers have to learn how to make sure that the best argument wins, not the most aggressive member of the group. One lesson that Burger tries to get across is that managers should solicit a range of opinions before making a decision, from experts, from younger executives, from customers. Engineer-managers do not necessarily need to be experts in every field of business, but, Burger says, they need "to speak the languages of those other functional areas. They need to ask the right questions."

The engineering excellence that makes German companies so successful has other hazards. There is such a thing as too much engineering, like the screws in the Siemens mobile phones that the company manufactured itself. That level of quality made the product far too expensive for the market. Therefore, another thing that ESMT teaches engineers is to make sure that there is actually a market for their exquisitely crafted products, to master the balance between perfectionism and salability. That may seem obvious, but it is not necessarily clear to an engineer. "In the 1990s German products were over-engineered," Rocholl, the ESMT president, says. "The products had everything, but no one wanted to buy them anymore. They pleased the engineer and not the customer." Rocholl, who teaches finance, tries to impress on students "not to concentrate so much on the product itself but also the utility that comes with it."

ESMT gives courses in both English and German, and attracts many students from China as well as other up-and-coming countries like Malaysia who want to learn German ways. The school does not enroll many Americans. Asians "want to understand the success factors of Germany," says Burger, who notes that the students are highly motivated and fast learners who may well challenge German dominance in engineering businesses. Indeed, he is worried about what will happen as foreign competitors begin to target niche markets occupied by German companies, and how long the German success story will last. The evidence suggests that the most successful manufacturing companies are those managed by people whose expertise in engineering is combined with a broader view of business, including finance, marketing, and design. The country with the most competitive economy is likely to be the one that breeds the best all-round managers. That country could be Germany, but it could also be a country like China, Korea, Brazil, or the United States. "Write your book fast," Burger told me, with a laugh.

13

The Seeds of Complacency (II)

My neighborhood florist does not look very much like a criminal. A gentle guy with a shaved head, you can see him mornings wearing an apron, clipping the stems of fresh roses or freesia in his small shop on a side street. But he almost ran afoul of the law a few years ago, on Mother's Day no less. His crime: setting up a placard on the sidewalk outside his shop advertising that he would stay open from 9 a.m. to 4 p.m. A city inspector happened by and warned that it was illegal to stay open so long on a Sunday, Mother's Day or not. Close earlier or be fined, the inspector warned.

For all its industrial prowess, there is another side to the German economy, one that suffers from some of the same overregulation and sclerosis usually associated with much more troubled European countries like Italy or Greece. This economy is overregulated, intended to insulate insiders from competition and deeply resistant to change. During the Eurozone crisis that began in 2010, Germany's chancellor, Angela Merkel, often scolded countries like Spain, Italy, and Greece to become more competitive. But the German economy features some of the same flaws that they do, including protected professions and zoning laws that favor existing businesses over new ones. Shopping hours have been liberalized in recent years—after an endless national debate—but restrictions remain in many places. "On special days, I don't think one should watch the clock so closely," my local florist griped a few months after his brush with the law, still sore about the lost sales of Mother's Day bouquets.

The revival of the industrial sector in Germany was the result of a combination of government policy, cooperation with organized labor, and the energy and ingenuity of people like Norbert Reithofer, Martin Kannegiesser, and other people we have met on previous pages. Unfortunately, the solid performance of Germany's economy has sapped the political will to address remaining flaws in the economy, and could lead to a competitiveness gap in the future. There is still a lot that could wrong with the German success story.

Germany's renaissance will not be complete until it takes the final steps needed to create a more flexible, dynamic economy.

"Germany has what I would call a dual economy," Andreas Wörgötter, a senior economist at the Organization for Economic Cooperation and Development (OECD) in Paris, told me in 2012. "On one side, we have this very dynamic, innovative, competitive and refreshingly unsubsidized export sector. On the other side, there is a much less glamorous services sector which depends on barriers to entry, subsidies, and not developing and reaching out for new activities."[1] Mr. Wörgötter oversaw an OECD report in 2012 that estimated Germany could add about 10 percent to growth over the following decade if it removed barriers to competition and other inefficiencies.[2] Surprisingly, the untapped potential in Germany was almost as high as that in Italy and higher than that in Spain, according to the OECD, an indication that the German domestic economy is not as superior to its southern neighbors as is often assumed. But it does not appear that German political leaders paid much attention to the OECD's advice.

Germans are justifiably proud of their ranking as the world's third-largest exporter. But Germany's large trade surpluses are, in many ways, the sign of an imbalanced economy. The nation ended 2012 with a current account surplus of 188.3 billion euros, up from 158.7 billion euros in 2011.[3] Instead of flowing back to the domestic economy, where it would benefit personal incomes and consumer spending, that substantial sum of money flowed abroad—and not always to good effect. In the years leading up to the financial crisis that began in 2008, German banks invested some of the country's surplus in Greek bonds, securities tied to the U.S. mortgage market, and other investments that promised better returns than safe German government bonds—and later went badly wrong. As a result of this massive misallocation of assets, German banks later became major enablers of the financial crisis and required a bailout larger than the one provided to U.S. banks.[4]

Germany's banking system is another glaring weakness in the national economy, and a source of risk. All the values that exemplify Germany's best industrial companies—prudence, caution, the patience to take the long view—seem to be missing from German financial institutions. Several of the managers profiled in this book said bluntly that they do not trust banks, a rather damning verdict from people who should be prime customers.

Much of the weakness in German banking is structural. About 45 percent of the German banking industry is in one form or another under political control.[5] The so-called *Sparkassen*, more than 400 local thrift institutions, dominate consumer and small-business lending and are usually overseen by the local mayor or another local politician. The six large *Landesbanken*, which handle larger loans and transactions, are also under the control of elected officials. The Landesbanken are typically owned by state governments along with groups of Sparkassen. The Sparkassen, it must be said, came through the financial crisis fairly unscathed. They follow an old-fashioned business model, collecting deposits and making loans. But the degree of political influence in the Sparkassen is at odds with Germany's self-image as a free-market economy, and poses a constant threat that capital will be allocated to the most politically connected enterprises rather than the best managed. History has shown that small banks can also cause financial crises. Witness the U.S. savings and loan debacle in the 1970s and 1980s. There is no guarantee that the Sparkassen will not be the source of some future financial crisis, either. As a group, the Sparkassen have pledged to cover each other's losses, which means that the failure of one of them could quickly infect the others.

The Landesbanken have a long history of corruption and mismanagement that has cost taxpayers tens of billions of euros. At this writing, six former managers of HSH

Nordbank, a Landesbank in Hamburg, are on trial for fraud and concealing the bank's dismal financial state. Meanwhile, several former managers of BayernLB, a Landesbank in Munich, are under investigation for insider trading, and were also responsible for bad investments that required a 10 billion euro bailout financed by taxpayers. BayernLB's former chief risk officer is in jail after being convicted of accepting a $44 million bribe from Bernie Ecclestone, the chief executive of the Formula One auto racing series. (Ecclestone, accused of making the payoff in 2006 so that the bank would sell its stake in Formula One to his favored buyer, has said he did nothing illegal.) Yet another Landesbank, WestLB in Düsseldorf, disappeared from the market altogether following losses in part from investments in the U.S. subprime market. WestLB was once one of Germany's largest lenders, with offices all over the world and ambitions to become a global investment bank.

Despite this disastrous history, the debate about the future of the banking system in Germany is "alarmingly non-intense," says Jörg Rocholl of the European School of Management and Technology (ESMT) business school. Because they are so intertwined with politics down to the grass-roots local level, the Sparkassen and the Landesbanks are a formidable political force. All the German political parties, from the business-oriented Free Democrats to the post-Communist Left Party, have a stake in the status quo, and there is no visible constituency for change. On the contrary, the impulse of German political leaders has been to resist efforts at the European level to unify the Eurozone's patchwork system of banking supervision. The Eurozone debt crisis was amplified by the tendency of national regulators to go easy on their domestic banks.

Germany's commercial banks have not exactly covered themselves in glory either. Mayer Amschel Rothschild of Frankfurt's Jewish ghetto founded the Rothschild banking dynasty in the eighteenth century and helped define modern banking. Deutsche Bank and others provided the financing for the industrialization of Germany in the nineteenth century. But in the twentieth century, Germany's big banks cooperated zealously with the Nazis and purged Jewish employees. A subsidiary of Dresdner Bank (since absorbed by Commerzbank) even played a role in building Auschwitz.[6] More recently, German banks have been guilty mostly of gross mismanagement and recklessness. The German federal government rescued Commerzbank after ill-advised investments that included Greek bonds and loans to the international shipping industry, shortly before the oceangoing cargo business sunk into a years-long depression. Deutsche Bank avoided an official bailout after the failure of U.S. investment bank Lehman Brothers in 2008, but took billions in write-offs and was helped indirectly by the U.S. government's rescue of insurer AIG., from which it had bought credit insurance. In common with the Landesbanks, Deutsche Bank suffers from criticism that it is too dependent on borrowed money. In 2013, Germany's largest banks borrowed on average 50 euros for every 1 euro of their own money, according to the Bundesbank. Economists considered this degree of leverage to be dangerously high.[7] German as well as French banks were significantly more leveraged than their Spanish or Italian counterparts, despite stereotypes of Teutonic prudence and Mediterranean dolce vita.[8]

German *Mittelstand* managers often speak with pride of how they avoid debt and finance expansion by living modestly and plowing profits back into the business. This is certainly admirable, but no modern economy can function without credit and a reasonably efficient banking system. That is especially true in Germany, where banks remain the main source of credit, in contrast to the United States, where businesses are more likely to issue stock or corporate bonds. Germany has not had a credit crunch because international money market funds regard the nation as a safe haven, and were willing to lend to German banks despite their problems. But if there was ever a crisis of confidence—triggered, for example, by the failure of one of Germany's overly leveraged banks—the German economy would be vulnerable, and its industrial base could also suffer.

Germany's capital markets also remain underdeveloped. Despite efforts to encourage risk capital, money for new ventures is almost pitifully small. In 2012, total venture capital in Germany was just 521 million euros, less than a tenth of the amount available in the United States—per quarter.[9] Historically, German entrepreneurs have managed to grow without access to venture capital, often by building on the foundations of existing businesses. But Germany also has a history of inventing things that are then exploited by others. The MP3 technology that makes music downloads over the Internet possible was invented by researchers at a branch of the Fraunhofer Society, the network of research institutes. But most of the revenue from online music flows to those who figured out how to market it, notably Apple.

The preponderance of family-owned companies is certainly one of the Germany economy's strengths—95 percent of German companies belong to families or individuals. Their wealth and prestige is inseparable from that of the company and they have a strong incentive to manage prudently, with an eye to the long-term health of the company rather than short-term profit. Count Anton-Wolfgang von Faber-Castell, owner of pencil and pen maker Faber-Castell, founded by an ancestor of the count's in 1761, expresses a sentiment typical of family managers. "I consider what I got from my father as a kind of fiduciary property, which in a way does not belong to me," the count told me in 2013.[10]

But not everyone can inherit a machine-tool maker or an auto parts supplier. Obviously, any modern economy must foster start-up companies. Germany continues to score poorly on several measures of its conduciveness to business start-ups. Bureaucratic obstacles are still relatively high and financing scarce.[11] In particular, a more abundant supply of venture capital would increase the chances that the German economy would benefit from German inventiveness.

The weakness of German banks and the hurdles to small-scale entrepreneurship help explain why Germany's domestic economy is notoriously torpid. Normally a dramatic plunge in unemployment of the kind Germany experienced after 2005 would trigger a surge in consumer spending and a boom in retail sales. That has not been the case. Retail trade in Germany in June 2013 was only 1.4 percent above what it had been in 2010, adjusting for inflation.[12] The country has been something of a graveyard for retailers. Walmart spent nearly a decade trying to break into the German market before finally giving up in 2006. Walmart! Catalog retailer Neckermann, once a German institution, folded in 2012.

There were many reasons for tepid consumer spending, including an aging population focused on saving for retirement, feelings of insecurity caused by the Eurozone debt crisis, and slow wage growth. But one important reason was the lack of a vibrant domestic services sector.

The barriers to entrepreneurship in Germany are often obscure, but cumulatively act as a significant drag on job creation and investment. For example, until 2013 intercity long-distance bus service was effectively prohibited in Germany. The decades-old ban shielded the government-owned rail company, Deutsche Bahn, and was dismantled only after a long political tug of war. Companies such as Deutsche Touring, a bus company based in Frankfurt, could offer direct service to foreign cities like Istanbul or Belgrade, Serbia. But until 2013 they were not allowed to operate domestic lines to, say, Munich. As soon as restrictions were lifted, the company began offering cut-rate service. A ticket to Berlin, for example, cost 39 euros—a price that Deutsche Bahn immediately matched. It was an example of the kind of vibrant competition that simultaneously lowers prices and creates jobs.

To be fair, Germany has made huge progress in the last decade toward removing strictures on the economy. In the 1990s, stores closed at 6:30 p.m. and were open only a few hours on Saturday morning—a nightmare for working parents. I speak from personal experience. Back in 1995 when my daughter was a newborn and my wife and I were living in Stuttgart, we ran out of diapers one Sunday. Desperate, we went to the train station, where shops were allowed to remain open. There we found a store clerk selling single disposable diapers from a drawer behind the cash register at black market prices. After a seemingly endless debate that pitted church leaders and labor unions against retailers, shop hours were gradually liberalized and now German states can decide their own rules. Most have lifted restrictions during the workweek, though Sunday is still taboo in most places. Florists and bakeries are typically allowed to open a few hours on Sunday.

Germany has in recent years eased strict licensing rules that required years of qualification even for professions like basket weaver or violin maker. But prolonged training is still required to qualify as a house painter, chimney sweep, or bicycle mechanic, to name a few examples. This is the negative side of Germany's obsession with *Ausbildung,* of creating a formal course of study for every profession, and making it impossible to get a job without the proper certificate. The OECD has called on Germany to loosen restrictions on advertising and fees, which limit competition among architects, lawyers, and engineers.

Almost every company profiled in this book has profited from the rise of China, and generally from the emergence of countries like Brazil or Russia as relatively open markets with growing affluence. In the case of BMW and Trumpf, China has become indispensable, providing the growth that is missing from traditional markets in Europe. In Germany, nervousness about the fate of the Chinese economy is palpable. In 2013, the Chinese economy was in an awkward phase. A new government was trying to find its way. After years of breakneck growth driven by exports, Chinese policymakers were trying to build stronger domestic demand, but seemed unsure how to do so. Economists worried about credit bubbles in China, and there had been massive overinvestment in sectors such as steel, mining, and cement production, resulting in a glut of capacity. This was a direct threat to Germany, which has many companies that supply equipment for steelmaking, mining, and cement production, or help build new plants. Some German managers were beginning to worry openly, such as Joe Kaeser, who took over as chief executive of Siemens in July 2013 after his predecessor was blamed for a slump in sales and profit. Siemens had expected the Chinese economy to rebound after the new government found its footing, Kaeser told reporters at a press conference at company headquarters in Munich. But it was becoming clear that China faced painful structural changes, with potential for civil unrest, and might not be as reliable a source of growth as it had been. "China clearly needs longer than we originally thought," Kaeser said.

Long term, Chinese sales may be less of a worry for German companies than Chinese competition. China is already the largest producer of machine tools in the world by a wide margin. But it has not yet become a serious threat at the specialized, high end of the market occupied by the likes of Trumpf. Chinese engineers are adept at producing copies that compete on price, but have not yet shown they can produce innovations for which customers are willing to pay a premium. Perhaps they never will. Some product niches are so narrow, and the cost of acquiring expertise so great, that it may not be worth the bother. Will any Chinese (or Brazilian or South African) entrepreneur ever aspire to produce high-quality museum display cases for export that would pose a threat to Glasbau Hahn in Frankfurt? Perhaps not, but German executives are certainly watching very closely to see where China's legions of capable, ambitious engineers decide to apply their energies. "In the short run they are still in a phase where they copy individual machines," Martin Kannegiesser says. It will take some time before the Chinese are global competitors in high-end machinery, Kannegiesser says, but he believes Chinese companies have the capability. "Putting it together into systems with a complete support system behind it worldwide, this will be possible. It cannot be excluded—they are intelligent." He adds, "We should not use the time factor as an excuse."

Franz Schabmüller, the auto components entrepreneur in Ingolstadt, and many other employers would like to see further reforms to German labor rules, which are less onerous than in France or Italy, but still discourage companies from hiring. It is very difficult for political leaders to explain to voters that reductions in job protections might help economic growth and lead to more and better jobs. Because there is no job crisis, there is no impetus for the kind of cooperation between labor, business, and government that took place in the early 2000s. The burden of labor flexibility falls disproportionately on temporary workers, who are the first to be fired in a crisis. In effect there is a two-tier labor force made up of those with relatively secure jobs and those who can be dismissed at any time. Because temp workers tend to be younger, there is a danger that youth unemployment would soar in the event of a serious crisis, which is what has happened in Greece and Spain, putting a severe strain on society. "If we had more liberal labor rules we wouldn't need to use so much temporary labor," Schabmüller says. "But you would never get that through in Germany. We'll never have labor rules like the United States."

One prominent economist even goes so far as to argue that Germany's success as an exporter has more to do with low wages than innovative manufacturers. Cuts in the cost of labor "have been the basis of the nation's export success in recent years," Adam Posen, president of the Peterson Institute for International Economics in Washington, wrote in the *Financial Times* in September 2013. "Low wages are not the basis on which a rich nation should compete."[13] Posen, who previously was a member of the rate-setting Monetary Policy Committee at the Bank of England, argues that German manufacturing is overrated. He cites data that factory jobs as a share of total employment have fallen by about the same amount in almost all advanced economies including Germany. I disagree with his analysis—a country does not get to be the world's third-largest exporter solely by paying people less. In any event, German industrial wages remain higher than those in the United States and are many multiples of what Chinese workers earn. So it is hard to see how German wages provide an explanation for the company's success in exports.

But Posen's criticism was taken seriously by German economists, even if they disagreed. Jörg Zeuner, chief economist of the Kreditanstalt für Wiederaufbau, a government-owned development bank that provides financing to German Mittelstand companies, argues that, while it is true manufacturing has declined as a proportion of the total economy, industry-related services have increased. A company like Herbert Kannegiesser, for example, not only makes equipment for industrial laundries but helps customers like the Sochi Olympics set up new laundries. Kannegiesser even helps customers organize transport of soiled clothing and bedsheets to the laundry and back to the customers' customers. Services are part of what allows German industrial companies to charge a premium and pay their workers relatively high wages, Zeuner says, but may not be counted as manufacturing for statistical purposes. In addition, German benefits from the presence of deep networks of industrial companies, not just automakers, for example, but vast numbers of Mittelstand suppliers that work closely together. "We do have the entire production in Germany, which is one big advantage," Zeuner says.[14]

But even if Posen is wrong about a decline in German industry, he makes an important criticism, one shared by Zeuner and many other economists. Germany is not investing enough in infrastructure or in education. At all levels of government, there is not enough spending on universities, schools, bridges, roads, sewage treatment plants, and other public infrastructure even to maintain them at current levels. In other words, the country's physical plant is slowly deteriorating. This is especially true in regions like the Ruhr Valley, Germany's rust belt, where big employers like Opel have been cutting jobs, and communities have been losing tax revenue. The situation is better in wealthier regions like Bavaria and Baden-Württemberg, but taxpayers there are becoming less willing to subsidize poorer regions. "On an aggregate level, net public investment is negative," Zeuner told me in 2013. "This is not good."

If Germany created a more efficient services sector, and were less dependent on exports, it also would become less vulnerable to the economic ups and downs of major markets like America and China. Ulf M. (Mark) Schneider, chief executive of Fresenius, a German health-care company that is the world's largest provider of dialysis products and services, worries in particular about Germany's dependence on the auto industry. But it could also be said that Germany has become spoiled by the success of its manufacturers in general, not only the giant household names like Daimler and Siemens but also the lesser-known Mittelstand companies like Bollin Armaturenfabrik or Glasbau Hahn. "If there was a more resilient domestic economy, it would at least cushion things a little bit," Schneider told me in 2012. "As great as the export performance is, we forget that we had a significant growth problem for 15 years before the financial crisis," said Schneider, who has dual U.S. and German citizenship, studied at Harvard Business School, and is able to see the German economy in a global context. "If any of these stories come to an end, we are as exposed as anyone."[15]

German leaders risk slipping into the same state of complacency that afflicted past generations. They must become more attentive to the danger.

14

Lessons for the Rest of the World

The ideal German company embodies traditions of craftsmanship, family loyalty, and vocational education that go back centuries, married to modern technology that enables instant communication and fast movement of people and things around the globe. The question is whether the model, and not just the products, can be exported to America and other places. Ask German managers that question, and you will encounter some skepticism. "In America you can do almost everything," Martin Kannegiesser replied when I asked him whether it would be possible to build a company like his in America. "The population is so dynamic. Everything is possible," he said. But then he added, "It will take a long time. This is a culture that has developed over generations," he said, referring to German traditions.

Berthold Leibinger of Trumpf questions whether Americans have enough appreciation for quality, the compulsive desire to manufacture things as perfectly as possible. "I always hear from Americans, 'I bought this other machine and it's not as good as yours, but it's good enough,'" Leibinger said. As an example of the different mentalities, he cited his condominium in Connecticut, near the Trumpf factory in Farmington. It is in a beautiful setting, he said, but the quality of the construction is "lousy." (As the former owner of a Connecticut condo myself, I know what he's talking about.) He thinks Americans are too focused on making money as quickly as possible. Whenever he was in the United States, people always wanted to know when he was going to sell shares in Trumpf, a transaction that could have made Leibinger a billionaire, but that he considers unthinkable for a company like his.

Leibinger, who as a young man was awestruck by the Cincinnati Milling Co., has watched the decline of the U.S. machine-tool industry with what appears to be genuine sadness. The state of Baden-Württemberg, with about 10 million people, makes more machine tools than all of

the United States, he said. "Why?" he asked. "It's not innovation. Americans are raised to have little respect for the
established order. They question things." He also admires
Americans' willingness to give people second chances, and
the way Americans can go bust, yet dust themselves off and
try again. "We have a weakness," Leibinger said of Germany.
"As a founder of a company you're not allowed to fail. In
America, you are." Leibinger also speaks highly of American
workers, their enthusiasm and engagement. If Americans
combined Teutonic attention to quality with their innovative gifts, he says, they would be formidable.

Certainly it is true that the German mindset that has
evolved over centuries is not so easy to box up and FedEx
to Ohio. But many of the elements that make German companies successful could be applied elsewhere by someone
with patience and determination. And America has many
advantages that German managers envy, like labor flexibility and cheap energy. In closing this book, let us reconsider
what allows German companies to continue to succeed in
manufacturing despite the obstacles they face, and what it
would take to replicate these elements elsewhere.

An international orientation. There is, alas, plenty of truth
to the stereotype that German businesspeople are more
international than their American counterparts. In 2012,
Germany exported goods and services worth $1.408 tril-
lion, rivaling exports from the United States, which were
worth $1.547 trillion.[1] Excluding services, Germany was
ahead of the United States even though it has about one-
quarter the population. Germans have to be international
because of the limits of their domestic economy; Americans do not, because their economy is the world's largest.
But highly specialized companies need global markets. For
a highly focused, technology-oriented company, even the
U.S. market may be too small to generate enough revenue
to support the amount of research and development (R&D)
that is required to stay ahead of the competition.

Exports by small and medium-size enterprises in the United States are growing. The number of U.S. companies that sold goods abroad rose more than 3 percent in 2011 to more than 300,000 firms, of which 98 percent had fewer than 500 employees—the American Mittelstand, if you will. That is the good news. The bad news, according to a study by the U.S. Department of Commerce, is that U.S. companies tend to export to only one foreign country, and that country is likely to be Canada.[2] What is more, U.S. companies tend to manage their exports from home rather than opening representative offices, or even opening manufacturing centers, abroad, as German companies commonly do. In other words, U.S. exporters tend to lack the international sophistication of their German competitors.

German companies show that there is no particular magic to operating globally. It is mostly a matter of deciding to do it, of having the courage to venture beyond the familiar, and the ingenuity to deal with unexpected situations. Judging from the German experience, specific business knowledge seems to be less important than a spirit of adventure and tolerance for foreign cultures. People like Till Hahn of Glasbau Hahn and Berthold Leibinger of Trumpf demonstrate the importance of travel as an element in the shaping of a modern manager. Hahn and Leibinger crisscrossed America as young men, so that today they feel comfortable in foreign places. Americans actually have a built-in advantage operating internationally because they already speak English, the lingua franca of global business. But it would not hurt to develop fluency in a widely spoken foreign language. That could be German, French, or Spanish, but with so much growth taking place in developing markets, it might make more sense for a young person today to study a language like Mandarin, Portuguese (for doing business in Brazil), Arabic, Swahili, or Hindi.

A strong emotional connection to the businesses. Many of the executives profiled in this book took over family businesses that they had grown up with, and for which they felt a strong attachment and sense of responsibility. Indeed, 95 percent of all German companies with fewer than 500 employees are family owned, and 85 percent are managed by the owner.[3] But Berthold Leibinger, initially an outsider in Trumpf, shows that you do not have to inherit a company to identify with it. More important is for a manager to find something he or she cares about, something that provides intrinsic satisfaction beyond the financial reward. The German managers in this book, and many others whom I have met over the years, take a palpable joy in making things. They look at a machine or a car coming off the factory floor and say to themselves, "Me and my people built that, and it's good!" Money is important, to be sure, but it is not what gets them out of bed in the morning. They take pleasure and pride in creating livelihoods for the people who work for them, in supporting their local economies, and above all in creating an institution that will outlive them.

Innovation. America is a nation of innovators, as Leibinger says. But innovation is not just about ideas. Innovation means being willing to invest a large chunk of revenue in R&D even when business is lousy. It means being patient if the payoff does not come right away. For publicly listed companies, being innovative means being able to explain to shareholders why it might make sense to contribute a large share of profits to R&D rather than dividends. For privately held companies, managers need the courage to keep investing in the future even when business is bad.

Occupying the high end of the market. This means making a product that customers are willing to pay more for, so that cost is not the decisive selling point. Being *premium* is closely tied to *perfectionism*, a compulsion to offer the highest level of quality and craftsmanship. This is a characteristic that seems to be implanted in Germans from a young age. German teachers are notoriously tough graders, and it is unusual for students, even the most brilliant, to earn the equivalent of straight As. Germany honors craftsmanship by rewarding years of apprenticeship and training with the title of *Meister*. But Germany owns no patent on perfectionism. Apple, the most successful American company of recent years, was the creation of a legendary perfectionist, Steve Jobs, who insisted that even the interior workings of his computers should look beautiful even though few customers would ever see them.

A cooperative relationship with employees. American companies, it is safe to say, do not like labor unions. And because American labor law is not very union-friendly, they do not have to like them. In Germany, almost any company with more than a few dozen workers is likely to have an employee council with a right to be consulted on major changes in working conditions. With no choice but to deal with workers, German managers have learned to use employee councils as a forum to get workers to buy into the program. The legal requirements aside, German companies have a strong incentive to retain their people, because of their dependence on highly skilled workers and their investment in training.

So here is a radical idea: what if American companies created employee councils even if they did not need to? I am well aware this suggestion will be met with incredulity in America. Give workers a committee, and the next thing you know they will want to be doing collective bargaining! When Volkswagen floated the idea of establishing a German-style workers council at its plant in Chattanooga, the governor of Tennessee accused the company of undermining the state's efforts to attract investment. Some American companies do seem to be grasping the wisdom of consulting employees. My own employer, the *New York Times*, has an internal employee forum, a combination suggestion box and social network, that mines workers for fresh ideas. Would it be so terrible, for example, to appoint lower-level employees to sit in on high-level management meetings and allow them to express their opinions about company strategy?

Another German innovation that could be imported to America is the work-time account, where workers bank overtime in the form of hours rather than cash. When times are slow, they work fewer hours, but take home the same pay by drawing from the work-time accounts. The system makes it easier for companies to hold onto their workers during a temporary downturn, preserving the investment that has been made in their training. And of course, it spares workers the trauma of unemployment. I understand there may be legal obstacles to setting up workers councils or work-time accounts in the United States, but these should not be insurmountable.

Managing for the long term. If your aim is to get rich quickly, manufacturing is probably not the business for you. At least that is the lesson from German companies. The trend for private equity companies to buy manufacturers and delist them from the stock market seems to be a tacit acknowledgement that subservience to quarterly earnings reports is not ideal for all firms. It takes patience and determination to build something that will last, to invest in innovation when times are tough, and to keep paying the best employees even when there is not enough work. A company that manages for the long term insists on quality, even when a competitor temporarily steals sales with a lower-priced product. Why are the top three premium car brands in the world—BMW, Mercedes, and Audi—all German? Because they understood that premium brands take decades to build, and never gave in to the temptation to cheapen their products (or they regretted it if they did—see DaimlerChrysler). If you manage for the long term, you may still get rich, but it could take a few decades. "What you need to get across to people is that it takes time," says Berthold Leibinger. "You have to be content with a rather ordinary life. You can't buy an airplane three years after you started your business."

The land of Bill Gates and Steve Jobs "doesn't need to import a founder mentality," Leibinger says. Nor does America need to import a passion for business and a taste for adventure. It may be that the most important elements of the reindustrialization of America already exist.

Notes

Introduction

1. German taxes equaled more than 37 percent of GDP by the end of the 1990s, compared to 30 percent in the United States. Organization for Economic Cooperation and Development (OECD), "Total tax revenue as percentage of GDP," table retrieved from: http://www.oecd.org/newsroom/41498733.pdf.
2. International Labour Organization, http://laborsta.ilo.org.
3. CIA World Factbook, https://www.cia.gov/library/publications/the-world-factbook/rankorder/2078rank.html.
4. Ernst & Young, 2013 Worldwide Corporate Tax Guide, http://www.ey.com/GL/en/Services/Tax/Worldwide-Corporate-Tax-Guide---XMLQS?preview&xml=~ec1mag es~taxguides~WCTG-2012~WCTG-DE.xml.
5. Jack Ewing, "German Steelworks Soars with Serra," *BusinessWeek*, July 9, 2007.
6. The company is now known as EEW Pickhan. The new owners no longer work for Serra, preferring instead to concentrate on the more profitable offshore platform business.
7. World Bank, http://databank.worldbank.org.
8. Jörg Asmussen, member of the executive board of the European Central Bank, speech delivered on June 23, 2013. http://www.ecb.int/press/key/date/2013/html/sp130623.en.html.
9. OECD, Total employment in manufacturing (table) http://www.oecd-ilibrary.org/industry-and-services/total-employment-in-manufacturing_20743882-table1.
10. Federal Labour Court, http://www.bundesarbeitsgericht.de/englisch/start.html.
11. World Economic Forum, Global Competitiveness Report 2013–2014, pp. 193, 194, 500–504 http://www3.weforum.org/docs/WEF_GlobalCompetitivenessReport_2013-14.pdf.
12. World Economic Forum, Global Competitiveness Report 2012–2014, p. 195.
13. World Economic Forum, Global Competitiveness Report 2012–2014, p. 383.

Chapter 1

1. Paul Erker, *Dampflok, Daimler, DAX: Die deutsche Wirtschaft im 19. und 20. Jahrhundert* (Stuttgart/Munich: Deutsche Verlags-Anstalt, 2001), 104.
2. Richard H. Tilly, *Vom Zollverein zum Industriestaat: Die wirtschaftlich-soziale Entwicklung Deutschlands 1834 bis 1914* (Munich, Deutscher Taschenbuch Verlag, 1990), 30.
3. Thyssen-Krupp website, http://www.thyssenkrupp.com/en/konzern/geschichte_grfam_k2.html.
4. Tilly, 102.
5. Siemens website, http://www.siemens.com/history/pool/perseunlichkeiten/gruendergeneration/werner_von_siemens_en.pdf.
6. Siemens website.
7. Erker, 64.
8. Tilly, 96–98.
9. Erker, 25.
10. Erker, 105.
11. Erker, 104.
12. Tilly, 86; Thyssen annual report 2012 (online version).
13. Tilly, 89.
14. Erker, 108.
15. Günther Quandt is also known to history as the first husband of Magda Ritschel, who later married Joseph Goebbels, for whom Adolf Hitler was best man.
16. Erker, 207.
17. Erker, 239.
18. Erker, 239.

Chapter 2

1. The Bertelsmann website, www.bertelsmann.de, chronicles the company's collaboration with the Nazis.
2. Berthold Leibinger, *Who Could Wish for Any Other Time But This: A Life Story* (Hamburg: Murman Verlag, 2010), 68.
3. Interview with Berthold Leibinger, July 11, 2103.
4. Reinhard Mohn obituary, *The Economist*, http://www.economist.com/node/14637283?story_id=14637283.

5. For a detailed history of Krupp, see William Manchester, *The Arms of Krupp* (Boston: Little, Brown, 2003).

6. Bertelsmann, official biography of Reinhard Mohn, http://www.bertelsmann.de/Bertelsmann/Geschichte/Reinhard-Mohn-%281921_2009%29.html.

7. *Encyclopedia Britannica*, Germany (online entry) http://www.britannica.com/EBchecked/topic/231186/Germany/58011/Economy#toc233608.

8. Leibinger, 41.

Chapter 3

1. Werner Abelshauser, *Deutsche Wirtschaftsgeschichte, von 1945 bis zur Gegenwart* (Munich: C.H. Beck, 2011), 366, 392.

2. Federal Statistical Office, https://www.destatis.de/DE/Zahlen-Fakten/GesamtwirtschaftUmwelt/VGR/Inlandsprodukt/Inlandsprodukt.html.

3. Karl Brenke, "Löhne in Ostdeutschland—Anpassung an das westdeutsche Niveau erst auf lange Sicht möglich." Deutsches Institut für Wirtschaftsforschung, Wochenbericht des DIW Berlin 24/01, 2001, http://www.diw.de/sixcms/detail.php/285767#HDR0.

4. Jan Schildbach, "German SMEs on a Sounder Financial Footing." Deutsche Bank Research, February 28, 2013, http://www.dbresearch.com/servlet/reweb2.ReWEB;jsessionid=0AB6ABAF3191D7929C5AEDAC1E12ACE9.srv-net-dbr-com?rwsite=DBR_INTERNET_EN-PROD&rwobj=ReDisplay.Start.class&document=PROD0000000000302455.

5. Jack Ewing, "The Decline of Germany." *BusinessWeek*, February 16, 2003, http://www.businessweek.com/stories/2003-02-16/the-decline-of-germany.

6. Jack Ewing, "Siemens Climbs Back." *BusinessWeek*, June 4, 2000, http://www.businessweek.com/stories/2000-06-04/siemens-climbs-back-intl-edition.

7. Jack Ewing, "The Fall of Leo Kirch." *BusinessWeek*, March 10, 2002, http://www.businessweek.com/stories/2002-03-10/the-fall-of-leo-kirch.

Chapter 4

1. Jack Ewing, "The Accidental Reformer." *BusinessWeek*, April 30, 2000, http://www.businessweek.com/stories/2000-04-30/gerhard-schroder-the-accidental-reformer-intl-edition.
2. German Federal Statistical Office, https://www.destatis.de/DE/ZahlenFakten/GesamtwirtschaftUmwelt/Verdienste Arbeitskosten/ArbeitskostenLohnnebenkosten/EUVergleich/Aktuell.html.
3. Deutscher Industrie- und Handelskammertag, "Mittelstand in Deutschland—Zahlen, Fakten, Selbstverständnis," Berlin, May 2013, pp. 4, 6, www.dihk.de.
4. Statistisches Bundesamt, Wiesbaden, monthly report on Insolvenzverfahren, March 2013, p. 3, https://www.destatis.de/DE/Publikationen/Thematisch/UnternehmenHandwerk/Insolvenzen/Insolvenzen2020410131034.pdf?__blob=publicationFile.
5. For a detailed chart of German unemployment, see Federal Statistical Office, https://www.destatis.de/DE/ZahlenFakten/Indikatoren/Konjunkturindikatoren/Arbeitsmarkt/arb210.html.

Chapter 5

1. Deutscher Industrie- und Handelskammertag, Mittelstand in Deutschland—Zahlen, Fakten, Selbstverständnis, Berlin, 2013, 17.
2. Institut der deutschen Wirtschaft Köln, "Mittelständische Forschungsmeister," iw-dienst (newsletter), March 3, 2011, p. 2.
3. Hermann Simon, *Hidden Champions: Lessons from 500 of the World's Best Unknown Companies* (Cambridge: Harvard Business School Press, 1996); Hermann Simon, *Hidden Champions of the 21st Century: Success Strategies of Unknown World Market Leaders* (London: Springer, 2009).

Chapter 6

1. Irma Kannegiesser died on September 2, 2013, at age 95.
2. Interview with Martin Kannegiesser, July 8, 2013.
3. Based on recollection of Martin Kannegiesser.

Chapter 7

1. Jack Ewing, "Germany's Export Prowess Weighs on Euro-Zone," *New York Times*, February 26, 2010.
2. Another member of the Hahn family, also named Otto, was awarded the Nobel Prize for chemistry in 1945.
3. Interview with Till Hahn and Isabel Hahn, May 28, 2013.
4. Creditreform, "Insolvenz in Deutschland," 1. Halbjahr 2013, p. 15, http://www.creditreform.de/Deutsch/Creditreform/Presse/Archiv/Insolvenzen_Neugruendungen_Loeschungen_DE/2013_-_1._Halbjahr/2013-07-04_Insolvenzen.pdf.

Chapter 8

1. Jack Ewing, "German Small Businesses Reflect Country's Strength," *New York Times*, August, 13, 2012.
2. Interview with Dagmar Bollin-Flade and Bernd Flade, June 10, 2013.
3. Creditreform, "Insolvenz in Deutschland," 1. Halbjahr 2013, p. 9, http://www.creditreform.de/Deutsch/Creditreform/Presse/Archiv/Insolvenzen_Neugruendungen_Loeschungen_DE/2013_-_1._Halbjahr/2013-07-04_Insolvenzen.pdf.

Chapter 9

1. Trump website, history time line, http://www.de.trumpf.com/uebertrumpf/geschichte/des-unternehmens.html.
2. Information for this section is drawn from an interview with Berthold Leibinger on July 11, 2103, and from his memoirs, *Who Could Wish for Any Other Time But This, A Life Story* (Hamburg: Murmann Verlag, 2010).
3. The 2012 World Machine-Tool Output & Consumption Survey, Gardner Publications, p. 2 http://www.gardnerweb.com/cdn/cms/uploadedFiles/World%20Machine%20Tool%20Output.pdf.
4. Berthold Leibinger, *Who Could Wish for Any Other Time But This*, 197–198.
5. Interview with Mathias Kammüller, July 11, 2013.

6. Press release, "Rekordwachstum bei Trumpf." October 19, 2011, http://www.trumpf.com/nc/de/presse/pressemitteilungen/pressemitteilung/rec-uid/84356.html.
7. Jack Ewing, "Europe's Economic Powerhouse Drifts East," *New York Times*, July 18, 2011.
8. Ewing, "Europe's Economic Powerhouse Drifts East."
9. Ewing, "Europe's Economic Powerhouse Drifts East."

Chapter 10

1. Norbert Reithofer, *Nutzungssicherung von Flexibel Automatisierten Produktionsanlagen* (Berlin: Springer Verlag, 1987).
2. Jack Ewing, "As BMW Is Put to the Test, Its Plans Are Years Ahead," *New York Times*, November 22, 2012.
3. Interview with Jürgen Maidl, June 20, 2013.
4. Ewing, "As BMW Is Put to the Test."
5. E-mail correspondence with Chris Bangle, October 20, 2012; October 21, 2012, and September 27, 2013.
6. Ernst & Young, "European Automotive Survey 2013," p. 16.
7. Ewing, "As BMW Is Put to the Test."

Chapter 11

1. Jack Ewing, "The Trade-Off That Created Germany's Job Miracle," *New York Times*, September 24, 2012.
2. Interview with Franz Schabmüller, September 5, 2012.
3. Interview with Christian Stöhr, September 6, 2012.
4. German Missions in the United States, "The German Vocational Training System: An Overview," http://www.germany.info/Vertretung/usa/en/06__Foreign__Policy__State/02__Foreign__Policy/05__KeyPoints/Vocational__Training.html.
5. Jack Ewing, "The Apprentice: Germany's Answer to Jobless Youth," *BusinessWeek*, October 7, 2009, http://www.businessweek.com/magazine/content/09_42/b4151033735128.htm.
6. Bundesagentur für Arbeit, "Der Arbeitsmarkt in Deutschland, Strukturen der Arbeitslosigkeit," p. 16, http://statistik.arbeitsagentur.de/Statischer-Content/Arbeitsmarktberichte/Berichte-Broschueren/Arbeitsmarkt/Generische-Publikationen/Strukturen-der-Arbeitslosigkeit-2012-05.pdf.

7. Ewing, "The Apprentice: Germany's Answer to Jobless Youth."
8. Ewing, "The Trade-Off That Created Germany's Job Miracle."
9. Ewing, "The Trade-Off That Created Germany's Job Miracle."
10. Ewing, "The Trade-Off That Created Germany's Job Miracle."
11. Handelsblatt, "Deutsche Berufsausbildung als Exportschlager," June 2, 2012, http://www.handelsblatt.com/unternehmen/management/strategie/us-arbeitsmarkt-deutsche-berufsausbildung-als-exportschlager/6476968.html.
12. Organization for Economic Cooperation and Development (OECD), "Education at a Glance, 2012," pp. 35–36, http://www.keepeek.com/Digital-Asset-Management/oecd/education/education-at-a-glance-2012_eag-2012-en.
13. See data from the Programme for International Student Assessment (PISA) studies conducted by the OECD, http://www.oecd.org/pisa/46643496.pdf.
14. Eurostat, http://epp.eurostat.ec.europa.eu/statistics_explained/index.php/Unemployment_statistics.
15. Ewing, "The Trade-Off That Created Germany's Job Miracle."
16. Mihály Fazekas and Simon Field, *A Skills beyond School Review of Germany* (Paris: OECD, 2013), 28.
17. Karl-Heinz Paqué, "Vollbeschäftigung wird Wirklichkeit," *Frankfurter Allgemeine Zeitung*, January 28, 2013, p. 18.
18. Ewing, "The Trade-Off That Created Germany's Job Miracle."

Chapter 12

1. Statistisches Bundesamt, "Nichtmonetäre hochschulstatistische Kennzahlen," Wiesbaden, 2012, p. 44, https://www.destatis.de/DE/Publikationen/Thematisch/Bildung-ForschungKultur/Hochschulen/KennzahlenNichtmonetaer2110431117004.pdf?__blob=publicationFile.
2. Brian L. Yoder, "Engineering by the Numbers; American Society for Engineering Education," p. 1, http://www.asee.org/papers-and-publications/publications/college-profiles/2011-profile-engineering-statistics.pdf.
3. United Nations Educational, Scientific, and Cultural Organization (UNESCO), "Students in Tertiary Education 2010,"

http://epp.eurostat.ec.europa.eu/statistics_explained/index. php/Tertiary_education_statistics.

4. World Economic Forum, "The Global Competitiveness Index 2013–2014," http://www3.weforum.org/docs/GCR2013-14/ GCR_Rankings_2013-14.pdf.

5. Graduate Management Admission Council, http://www.gmac. com/GMACWCMSite/s/DeansDigest/www.gmac.com/gmac/ newsandevents/deansdigest/2010/April2010/DTG.htm.

6. Volkswagen website, http://www.volkswagenag.com/content/ vwcorp/content/en/the_group/senior_management/winter-korn.html.

7. Daimler website, http://www.daimler.com/dccom/0-5-78470-1-56953-1-0-0-0-0-0-104-7145-0-0-0-0-0-0-0.html.

8. Interview, *ADAC Motorwelt*, February 2013, p. 30.

9. Berthold Leibinger, *Who Could Wish For Any Other Time But This, A Life Story* (Hamburg: Murmann Verlag, 2010), 320–321

10. Günther Rehme, "Wissen und Neue Wachstumstheorie: Die Rolle von fachspezifischem Humankapital," *Darmstadt Discussion Papers in Economics*, November 8, 2007.

11. Interview with Jörg Rocholl, August 26, 2013.

12. Interview with Christoph Burger, August 26, 2013.

13. Jack W. Brittain and Sim B. Sitkin, "Carter Racing," Delta Leadership Incorporated, Carrboro, NC, 2006.

Chapter 13

1. Jack Ewing, "In Germany, a Limp Domestic Economy Stifled by Regulation," *New York Times*, February 22, 2013.

2. Organization for Economic Cooperation and Development (OECD), "Economic Survey of Germany 2012," http://www. oecd.org/germany/economicsurveyofgermany2012.htm.

3. German Federal Statistical Office, https://www.destatis.de/ DE/ZahlenFakten/GesamtwirtschaftUmwelt/Aussenhandel/ Gesamtentwicklung/Aktuell.html.

4. European Commission, "State Aid in the Context of the Financial Crisis," http://ec.europa.eu/competition/state_aid/ studies_reports/ws7_1.xls

5. Bankenverband, Marktanteil der Bankengruppen, http://bankenverband.de/service/statistik-service/banken/marktanteile-der-bankengruppen.
6. For an exhaustive treatment of Dresdner Bank's role during the Nazi period, see Klaus-Dietmar Henke, *Die Dresdner Bank im Dritten Reich* (four volumes) (Munich: Oldenbourg Verlag, 2006). For an English-language summary, see http://www.spiegel.de/international/dresdner-bank-and-the-third-reich-hitler-s-willing-bankers-a-401575.html.
7. For more on German banks, and leverage issues in general, see Anat Admati and Martin Hellwig, *The Banker's New Clothes* (Princeton, NJ: Princeton University Press, 2013).
8. Jakob Vestergaard and María Retana, "Behind Smoke and Mirrors: On the Alleged Recapitalization of Europe's Banks," Danish Institute for International Studies, p. 44, http://www.isn.ethz.ch/Digital-Library/Publications/Detail/?ots591=0c54e3b3-1e9c-be1e-2c24-a6a8c7060233&lng=en&id=164542.
9. German Private Equity and Venture Capital Association, press release, February 25, 2013, http://www.bvkap.de/privateequity.php/cat/67/aid/814/title/BVK's_annual_statistics_for_2012:_a_strong_final_spurt_for_the_German_equity_capital_market; PricewaterhouseCoopers LLP (PwC) press release, April 19, 2013, http://www.pwc.com/us/en/press-releases/2013/venture-capital-investments-decline-in-dollars.jhtml.
10. Jack Ewing, "Hands-On Bavarian Count Presides Over a Pencil-Making Empire," *New York Times*, December 3, 2013.
11. See: World Economic Forum, "The Global Competitiveness Report 2012–2013," p. 177, Geneva, 2013, www.weforum.org.
12. Eurostat, "Volume of Retail Trade Down by 0.5% in Euro Area," August 5, 2013, http://epp.eurostat.ec.europa.eu/cache/ITY_PUBLIC/4-05082013-AP/EN/4-05082013-AP-EN.PDF.
13. Adam Posen, "Germany Is Being Crushed by Its Export Obsession," *Financial Times*, September 4, 2013, p. 7.
14. Interview with Jörg Zeuner, September 5, 2013.
15. Ewing, "In Germany, a Limp Domestic Economy Stifled by Regulation."

Chapter 14

1. Bundesministerium für Wirtschaft und Technologie, "Fakten zum deutschen Außenhandel 2012," Berlin, 5.
2. International Trade Administration, U.S. Dept. of Commerce, U.S. Exporting Companies 2011.
3. Bundesministerium für Wirtschaft und Technologie, "German Mittelstand: Motor der deutschen Wirtschaft," Berlin, 2012, 5.

Index

CPSIA information can be obtained
at www.ICGtesting.com
Printed in the USA
BVHW041007131220
595591BV00006B/82

9 781137 349736